HOW TO BE THE

(in a conflicted and cont rolling world)

By Nick Withycombe

Disclaimer

None of the contents of this or any other material by the author is intended as medical advice. Always seek certified professional guidance on matters of health.

Table of Contents

Foreword

Do you ever feel there is a 'most you' somewhere inside? This is the version of you that you see the most clearly. This you is the version you like the most. This you can achieve what you want to achieve. Be seen, heard and remembered. This you is untainted and uncorrupted by modern society.

But then things get in the way.

Society brings you negativity, manipulation, adrenaline, cortisol. Modern life ignites dopamine cravings. There's no time for you, there's no way to stop the rat race. The conflict and control keeps this 'you' trapped inside: daily basics, other people's needs, real life.

So you're told to 'do things'. Be healthy. Learn stuff. And ugh, *meditate* and be introspective. Journal!

You've dismissed, tried and stopped, got bored and failed, lost motivation.

This is because there has never been any pay off from any of these things.

From 5,000 years ago, humans already realised that mindfulness and introspection and zen-ish-ness were good. But they didn't stop the next 5,000 years from being what they were, and they haven't done lots for you so far.

So how else can you get what you want and be the most YOU in a world where you're surrounded by modern nonsense?

This isn't about being the 'best' you. Who wants to be at their best for every minute of the day?

This is about honouring one person, created in a flicker of a moment on planet Earth: that's you. You!

The only time you have is now.

The only mind and body you have is your own.

So let's make it time to be the most you.

Introduction

So what does 'the MOST you' mean?

What is this all about and what can you expect?

You know when you hear people reference Plato, and you think 'I should probably find out what Plato said,' but then you never do because who is actually going to read the Wikipedia entry of everything mildly interesting they've heard that day?

Well, history can be fun!

So through the sections of this book, we will take a look at key (interesting) things that famous people said in the past.

It's both nice to have this information in one's brain, and useful to know how us humans became quite so bizarre as we are, and what really clever people realised about our existential conundrum: of being creatures with animal urges but higher reasoning, AKA sentient meat.

After we look at what intelligent people have said about the topic, we have a baseline of context, i.e. what is the general idea of what is happening in our mind, related to the topic of who you are, why you act and what you want. Of course, we are all unique by definition, yet we are also all the same, by other definitions. We all stem from the same pool of ancestors (eventually) and we all live somewhere on Earth. We haven't changed that much - or at all - from hundreds or even thousands of years ago, from the general reality of being alive, living among other humans and having a path through life of birth, childhood, adulthood, elderliness and death.

What this means is that really intelligent people - let's stick with Plato in this example - thought up things that are still at the core of modern human life.

Freud's thoughts completely reframed the concept of the human mind at the time, although it was very much of the time. Separating the mind into the id, the ego and superego was ground-breaking, however, many of his other theories have become less relevant with time.

For the more recent 'thinkers', to be honest, they didn't really come up with such seminal, mind-blowing insights. Yet, it's still good for you (or anyone) to be aware of more recent, nuanced takes on the previous historical thinkers. Most people know about Maslow, and so it's helpful to learn about such ideas, yet we can also critique them, simply because they are based on very general assumptions.

Thus, we see that the path of thinkers starts with the key theories of human thoughts and existence being founded long ago, and becoming less and less 'key' over time. This is a natural process, akin to old inventions such as electricity being the foundation of modern existence, while the invention of the home bread-making machine, while useful for some, is more of a nuanced frivolity than a seminal revelation.

And yet! We will also look at things that have not yet been fully agreed upon, fully researched and fully accepted as commonly accepted reality. One example of this is synchronicity, another is telepathy. And so the path of your reading experience here shall be:

- The ground-breaking discoveries of human behaviour
- More recent thoughts that set the tone to culture and society, yet are more easily criticised and less famously accepted (but good to know)
- How any of this is affecting your ability to be the most you
- How we can apply these learnings into life
- Breaking it all down into what is ridiculous and what is revelatory

And the sections we will go through are:

1. Your mind
2. Your heart
3. Your gut
4. Your genitals
5. Living as the most you

Now, you've obviously already focused on the genitals there. This is included because most books or thoughts on health, mentality or overall wellbeing do not cover the area. The very important area. Of your genitals. Seriously and maturely, our hormones and urge to procreate are important aspects of the whole person and shouldn't be dismissed. Of course, the thoughts happen in the brain, but the heart refers to emotions, the gut refers to both the gut-brain axis and also intuition, and the genitals to our sex-brain axis.

We will look at how evolution, history, society, family and everything around you has and is forming your thoughts and feelings, and how much of it is stopping you from being the most you.

NOT the 'BEST' you

First off, who really wants to be their 'best' selves all the time, or even very often? It sounds like too much effort, doesn't it? It sounds like we have to save the world (or at least the small children) and use all of our energy and have ice cold showers and clean fingernails and flowery armpits and compassion.

Secondly, it's about you doing you. You may soon see that one personally thrills to more archaic prose, yet, 'you do you' is a powerfully succinct mantra. One of the main causes of depression is when people feel the need to put up a facade and try to make themselves look like someone they are really and truly not. This excellent point was explained by Jim Carrey, who will be referenced one further time in this book.

It's a reference that I've seen first-hand to be true. I knew a man who was depressed and my opinion was that it was all due to him wearing a facade of being successful, being knowledgeable, a master, a guru who would readily help and advise others. Yet, he disliked even asking for any help himself, let alone taking it. It didn't go along with the image he was trying to present to the world. That effort is so overly mentally tiring that it can be a cause of depression when the other part of the mind just can't keep it going.

If we categorise this in list format, here are five reasons why this isn't about being 'the best you':

1. Pressure and Perfectionism: Encouraging individuals to be their best self can create pressure and foster a perfectionistic mindset. It may lead to setting unrealistically high standards and expectations for oneself, which can be detrimental to mental health. The constant pursuit of perfection can result in self-criticism, fear of failure, and feelings of inadequacy.

2. Self-Judgment and Comparison: The emphasis on being one's best self can trigger self-judgement and comparison to others. When individuals constantly measure themselves against an idealised version of themselves or compare themselves to others, it can lead to feelings of dissatisfaction and diminished self-worth. It may also hinder self-acceptance and prevent individuals from appreciating their unique qualities and strengths.

3. Inauthenticity and Self-Denial: Striving to be one's best self may inadvertently lead to suppressing or denying certain aspects of one's true self. The pressure to conform to societal or internalised expectations of what being the best self entails can result in a lack of authenticity. This can create inner conflicts and a sense of disconnection from one's genuine desires and values.

4. Overemphasis on Achievement and External Validation: The notion of being the best self may place

excessive emphasis on external achievements, success, and validation. This can lead individuals to define their self-worth solely based on external factors such as accomplishments, wealth, or social status. Consequently, it may hinder the development of a healthy and balanced self-concept that includes other aspects of personal wellbeing and fulfilment.

5. Stress and Burnout: The relentless pursuit of being one's best self can contribute to chronic stress and burnout. When individuals constantly strive to meet high expectations and push themselves beyond their limits, it can lead to physical and mental exhaustion. This can impact overall wellbeing, relationships, and quality of life.

The premise of being the most you means looking at how self-acceptance, personal satisfaction and genuine fulfilment can help individuals navigate the potential negative aspects of society.

Not the most everything

Being the most you doesn't mean being at your loudest, most forthright or argumentative, going round your circle of existence and getting in people's faces.

The most you is a balance between urges, social expectations, real life, and the various selves that make up the whole you.

Taken in the context of a controlling and conflicted world, the idea is to continually imagine (and then perhaps become, if you like) the person you are. Not the person others want you to be, or the consumer that money-makers want you to be, or the economic unit that the government wants you to be, or the you that you think you *should* be.

Take away time and context and consider who you ARE, away from the era in which you live. What if you were born hundreds of years ago? Or in another country? Or with different people raising you? What is the you that creamly rises to the top of that milky mix?

Being the MOST you

Being the MOST you is an assumption of goodness. If you are a bad person then please throw this book away (you won't care where it lands) and only return to it when you are nice. Of course, I'm just kidding. You are reading a book and therefore chances are that you are good.

Thusly, being the MOST you means harnessing your goodness and unleashing your goodness and then feeling good about who you are and what you do. That level of positive goodness can only possibly ripple further goodness unto the world, and we will all be living in a better society, a better planet if good people feel capable and able to feel good.

We only get one life.

This is a truism that can unravel into the most extreme extremities of existentialism. If you have a spare moment, do feel free to start thinking about why we're here and why the universe is a thing (or is it even a thing?), but, it may be more expedient in your whole wellbeing journey thing if we just hold that dear: we only get one life.

That is the basis of our will to be our MOST selves; to make use of the gift that we have: life. It's a funny gift, we don't know why we were given it, but that's not important. This isn't like Christmas where nice gifts come with opposing obligations (you know, guilt/boredom/dis-satisfaction/let down/fatness), this is a free gift: to live!

Being the most you is just a nice way to live. Again, we go with assumptions: it's nice to feel confident, empowered, clear-minded, content, purposeful. It's nice to wake up in the morning with a pleasant day ahead, and it's nice to go to bed feeling that it was a good day.

That's important: the "I had a good day" concept, from the perspective of a good life and also good individual days. Any kind of self improvement or wish to 'achieve' often looks at big things, because they sound tempting: get a better career, totally change your appearance and the like. Being the most you can indeed change 'your life' but equally important are individual days; probably more important because you don't live 'your whole life' all in one go. All you have, when you boil it down, is each individual day to experience. Even if you 'get' things (the partner/job/house/car/holiday social expectation), then the things can become very boring, very quickly.

Simply having a good day is becoming less mentioned, as people only offer the highlight reel of their life.

So how do we live each day well? Let's find out over many interesting pages!

PART ONE
YOUR MIND

Your Mind

We start with the premise that it's odd to have a human mind.

Of course, we understand more about the mind now than in the past - but only up to a point.

Yes, the more that time goes on, the more science can tell us.

But what's interesting is that key foundations of how our funny minds work were realised hundreds nay thousands of years ago.

There is the 'higher' part of our mind, which drives humanity to be better.

There are also the base, animal parts that can be guilty of what we see as the 'bad' of the world.

And, there is everything in between.

So let's look at when and where previous humans realised the what and why of human minds.

We'll go from 5,000 years ago and quickly up to the present day. We'll note how simple things like mindfulness, introspection and self-reflection were already realised thousands of years ago, and then disappeared for several hundred years until they were brought back to life in recent times, re-packaged and then sold as poe-faced fixes for mental dis-satisfaction.

Ancient Texts

The exploration of ancient texts offers a unique window into the human condition, allowing us to trace the earliest realisations and articulations of human emotions. By analysing texts from various civilisations, including Mesopotamia, Egypt, India, and China, we can unravel the rich tapestry of emotions experienced by our ancestors and the insights they had, long before someone said it in an Instagram caption under a bum-photo of them wearing invasively tight yoga leggings.

Mesopotamian Literature: The Epic of Gilgamesh:

One of the oldest recorded texts, the Epic of Gilgamesh, composed in ancient Mesopotamia, provides valuable insights into the early recognition of human emotions. This epic poem, dating back to the third millennium BCE, recounts the adventures of Gilgamesh, a legendary king. Throughout the narrative, emotions such as grief, fear, anger, and joy are prominently portrayed, illustrating the complex emotional landscape of its characters. Notably, the portrayal of grief and mourning in response to the death of a loved one demonstrates an early understanding of profound emotional experiences.

Egyptian Wisdom Literature: The Maxims of Ptahhotep:

Egyptian wisdom literature, such as The Maxims of Ptahhotep, offers glimpses into ancient Egyptian perceptions of emotions. Ptahhotep, a vizier during the Old Kingdom of Egypt, authored this collection of moral and ethical teachings. While the text primarily focuses on virtues and ethical conduct, it also touches upon emotions and their impact on human behaviour. For example, Ptahhotep advises against acting impulsively out of anger, highlighting an awareness of the negative consequences of uncontrolled emotions. These insights reveal an early recognition of the need for emotional regulation and the importance of maintaining harmony within oneself and society.

Indian Philosophical Texts: The Vedas and Upanishads:

The ancient Indian texts, the Vedas and Upanishads, offer profound philosophical reflections on human emotions and their role in spiritual development. The Rigveda, one of the oldest Hindu scriptures, contains hymns that express a wide range of emotions, from praise and joy to fear and lamentation. The Upanishads, which delve into deeper metaphysical and philosophical concepts, explore the nature of emotions and their relationship to the self. For instance, the Brihadaranyaka Upanishad discusses the five sheaths (panchakoshas) that encapsulate human existence, including the emotional sheath (manomaya kosha). This exploration suggests an early recognition of the intricate interplay between emotions, consciousness, and spiritual growth.

Chinese Philosophical Texts: Confucianism and Taoism:

Chinese philosophical texts, particularly those of Confucianism and Taoism, provide significant insights into the understanding of emotions in ancient China. Confucius emphasised the cultivation of emotional harmony and virtuous conduct as crucial elements for maintaining social order and personal wellbeing. His Analects stress the importance of empathetic understanding, self-regulation, and the expression of appropriate emotions in various social contexts. Taoist texts, such as the Tao Te Ching, offer a contrasting perspective by advocating for emotional detachment and alignment with the natural flow of existence. These texts collectively reveal an awareness of the complexity of human emotions and the varying approaches to their management and expression.

Links to then and now:

These days, people talk about wellbeing terms as if they are new. They aren't, but they did go out of fashion for quite a long time - some hundreds of years.

The ancient Indian texts, the Vedas and Upanishads, were talking about things that you may see on social media currently, as if we've just realised them.

Here are the key pointers that were realised thousands of years ago in these texts:

Self-awareness and reflection: The Vedas and Upanishads emphasise the importance of self-awareness and introspection. Taking time to reflect on our thoughts, emotions, and actions can help us understand ourselves better and make conscious choices that align with our values and wellbeing.

4

Emotional intelligence: Understanding and managing our emotions is crucial for living well. The texts encourage us to cultivate emotional intelligence by recognizing, accepting, and appropriately expressing our emotions. Developing empathy and compassion towards others also fosters healthy relationships and a sense of interconnectedness.

Balance and moderation: The concept of "Sattva" in the Vedas refers to purity, harmony, and balance. It suggests cultivating a balanced lifestyle that encompasses physical, mental, and spiritual wellbeing. Finding a middle path between extremes and practising moderation in our daily routines, including work, rest, and recreation, can contribute to a more fulfilling and sustainable life.

Mindfulness and presence: The Upanishads talk about the importance of being fully present in the current moment. They say that practising mindfulness allows us to engage with our experiences, both mundane and profound, with clarity and attentiveness. It helps us appreciate the simple joys in life and reduces stress and anxiety caused by excessive preoccupation with the past or future.

Detachment and non-attachment: While actively participating in life, the texts suggest cultivating a sense of detachment from the outcomes of our actions. This doesn't imply apathy, but rather developing an attitude of non-attachment, where we focus on doing our best without being overly attached to the results. It helps us navigate challenges and setbacks with equanimity.

Seek knowledge and wisdom: The Vedas and Upanishads advocate the pursuit of knowledge and wisdom as a means of personal growth and self-realisation. Engaging in lifelong learning, exploring diverse perspectives, and seeking wisdom from various sources can expand our understanding of ourselves and the world around us.

Service and altruism: They note the importance of selfless service and contributing to the wellbeing of others. Engaging

5

in acts of kindness, generosity, and service to society fosters a sense of purpose, fulfilment, and interconnectedness with the larger community.

Taoist Texts

Taoist texts, particularly the Tao Te Ching, present a contrasting perspective to other philosophical and spiritual traditions by saying there is a concept of the natural flow of existence. Taoism is a Chinese philosophy that emphasises harmony with the Tao, which can be translated as "the Way" or the underlying principle of the universe.

In the context of Taoism, the natural flow of existence refers to living in accordance with the inherent harmony and rhythm of the universe. It suggests aligning oneself with the spontaneous and effortless unfolding of events, rather than resisting or forcing things to conform to personal desires or expectations. It recognizes that the world operates according to its own innate patterns and cycles.

Here are some key aspects of the natural flow of existence in Taoism:

Wu Wei (Non-Action): The concept of Wu Wei is central to Taoist philosophy. It does not mean literal inaction but rather refers to effortless action or action in alignment with the natural flow. It involves acting without unnecessary effort, allowing events to unfold naturally, and avoiding unnecessary interference or resistance.

Yin and Yang: The Tao Te Ching is about the interplay of Yin and Yang, the dualistic forces that represent complementary and interconnected aspects of the universe. Yin represents the feminine, receptive, and yielding qualities, while Yang represents the masculine, active, and assertive qualities. Harmonising these forces within oneself and in relation to the external world is seen as essential for living in harmony with the natural flow.

6

Embracing Simplicity: Taoist teachings often advocate simplicity and minimalism. By letting go of excessive desires, attachments, and ambitions, one can align with the natural flow. Simplicity allows for greater ease, contentment, and freedom from the burdens of material possessions and societal expectations.

Spontaneity and Intuition: Taoism encourages trusting one's intuitive wisdom and spontaneity. By quieting the mind and cultivating inner stillness, individuals can connect with their inherent wisdom and navigate life in a more intuitive and authentic manner.

Acceptance and Detachment: Taoist philosophy promotes acceptance of the present moment and detachment from specific outcomes. By releasing the need for control and surrendering to the natural course of events, individuals can experience greater peace of mind and harmony with the flow of existence.

Harmonising with Nature: Taoism is about the interconnectedness of humans and nature. By observing and aligning with the rhythms and patterns found in the natural world, individuals can attune themselves to the natural flow of existence.

The natural flow of existence in Taoism is not about passively accepting everything or being indifferent. It is about finding a balance between effort and non-effort, action and non-action, and harmonising with the underlying principles and energies of the universe. By doing so, individuals can cultivate a sense of inner peace, spontaneity, and harmony with the world around them.

What About the West?

It's important that we don't stereotype 'Eastern philosophy' or 'Western'. It becomes a selling point for people to try to describe 'Eastern' things as mythical and magical. Science, for example, is universal. Gravity works everywhere. Let's not be silly.

The issue is preconceived notions. Words like 'ayurvedic' and 'reiki' and 'vishwana' sound more exotic than 'eating an apple', and so people try to sell exotic sounding things as being good for health. Thus, you'll find little research done on how people in Britain talked about philosophies of health and wellbeing thousands of years ago. If it had a particular name that sounded kind of cool, you can bet that the Celtic or Druid notion of [esoteric name that doesn't sound modern] would be repackaged and sold today. It's a bit like they were out of Asian wording so they just turned to 'hygge' a few years ago, but most people just got bored of that.

The oldest particular clan of people in 'the West' were the druids, whom I suppose were a bit mythical, but didn't write any of it down. They (as far as historians know) lived in normal ways; farming, eating, procreating, existing in an abundant land with a temperate climate.

The oldest writing that's relevant to this whole topic might be "The Wanderer", an Old English poem that explores the search for meaning and stability in a world marked by transience and impermanence. The poem, written around 1,000 years ago, is written from the perspective of a lone survivor, an exile who has lost his lord and community, and it reflects on the struggles and sorrows faced by the wanderer.

In the poem, the wanderer describes his experiences of isolation, sorrow, and longing. He laments the impermanence of human relationships and the ephemeral nature of worldly joys. The wanderer acknowledges that the world is constantly changing, and nothing remains fixed or certain. He witnesses the ruins of great civilizations, reflecting on the inevitable passage of time and the fleetingness of human achievements.

Amidst this backdrop of transience and loss, the wanderer grapples with the search for meaning and stability. He contemplates the role of fate and destiny, recognizing that all

8

things are subject to the whims of fate and that one must accept the sorrows and hardships that come with it. The wanderer reflects on the concept of wyrd, the Old English word for fate or destiny, which implies an acceptance of life's trials and tribulations.

The poem also explores the idea of kinship and the importance of community. The wanderer mourns the loss of his lord and the disintegration of his social bonds. He longs for the warmth and security of his former home and the companionship of his fellow warriors. The poem highlights the human need for connection and stability, noting the pain and emptiness experienced when those bonds are severed.

Despite the melancholic tone of the poem, "The Wanderer" also contains a sense of resilience and endurance. The wanderer finds solace in the recollection of past glories and the memory of better times. He draws strength from his own inner resolve and the knowledge that worldly pleasures are fleeting. The poem suggests that true stability and meaning can be found in the acceptance of life's hardships and the pursuit of spiritual fulfilment.

"The Wanderer" explores the search for meaning and stability in a world marked by constant change and the inevitable passage of time. It reflects on the human condition, acknowledging the struggles and sorrows faced by individuals while also recognising the resilience of the human spirit in the face of adversity. The poem offers contemplation on the transitory nature of worldly pursuits and the enduring quest for a deeper sense of purpose and belonging.

More Modern Concepts:

So, in history, we have the basic understanding: we have a mind and need to understand it. Understanding it will allow us to move from the negative to the positive, and therefore increase comfort and control within the mind.

In between now and then, we have the renowned thinkers, such as Plato and then Freud. We will look at these (and other) key figures in the later sections of this book, as we refer to the different parts of the whole you, as mentioned in the introduction.

As we look at recent thoughts, this is a rapid change of gear. It's almost as if humans had their realisations many hundreds of years ago, but then weren't particularly interested in that anymore, so just went round warring in a chaos of bloodlust for many centuries.

The point is that 'the mind' and mental wellbeing is often talked about as if the mind is a delicate, spiritual thing that needs mindfulness - relentless mindfulness - and introspective thought. These things can be good, as we will look at later, but they are quite boring and also not new.

They are very much 'OK, what now?'.

This is where the contradiction of the human state is. The various parts of the mind-body make-up all need satiating, not only the delicate and tender mind.

So, let's first look at some people who look at our mind from the context of how it is positioned by external forces.

Noam Chomsky is known for exploring cognitive biases and their influence on political behaviour. He discusses how individuals, including those in positions of power, can be subject to confirmation bias, where they seek information that aligns with their preexisting beliefs, and ignore or dismiss evidence that contradicts their views. Chomsky suggests that these biases can contribute to self-serving decision-making and the perpetuation of unjust systems.

Additionally, Chomsky critiques the socialisation and cultural factors that shape individuals' perspectives and behaviours. He argues that dominant cultural norms and ideologies often prioritise individualism, consumerism, and material wealth over collective wellbeing and social justice. Chomsky calls for a critical examination of these cultural narratives and a reevaluation of societal values to foster a more equitable and just world.

Another important author is Naomi Klein. She argues that the concentration of power in the hands of corporations and the wealthy has significant implications for democracy and social justice. In her book "No Logo," she examined the rise of corporate branding and its impact on labour rights, consumer culture, and the erosion of public spaces. She contends that corporate interests have gained significant influence over politics, shaping policies that favour their own profits and priorities.

One of Klein's central arguments revolves around the concept of "disaster capitalism," as explored in her book "The Shock Doctrine." She posits that during times of crises, whether natural disasters or political upheavals, powerful actors exploit the chaos to advance their own agendas. She opines that governments often implement policies that further concentrate wealth and power, privatising public resources and dismantling social safety nets under the guise of economic restructuring.

Klein also addresses the role of neoliberalism in exacerbating power imbalances. She critiques the ideology that prioritises deregulation, privatisation, and unfettered free markets, arguing that it enables the concentration of power in the hands of a few while widening economic disparities. Klein highlights how neoliberal policies have led to austerity measures that disproportionately impact marginalised communities and contribute to social and economic inequalities.

In terms of accountability, Klein emphasises the need for transparency, public scrutiny, and citizen participation in decision-making processes. She criticises the influence of corporate lobbying and campaign financing on politics, which can result in policies that serve the interests of the wealthy elite rather than the broader population. Klein advocates for a more democratic system that prioritises the wellbeing of people and the planet over profit and corporate interests.

Life Imitating Art Imitating Life

It's not just 'a thought about society'.

Fiction is fueled by reality. There are several famous films and books that explore the concept of powerful elites controlling the mass population in various ways. Here are some notable examples:

Books:

"1984" (1949): George Orwell's dystopian novel. The story depicts a totalitarian society ruled by the Party, led by Big Brother, who monitors and controls every aspect of people's lives.

"Brave New World" by Aldous Huxley (1932): This novel presents a futuristic society in which the population is conditioned and controlled by a totalitarian government through technology, drugs, and social engineering.

"Fahrenheit 451" by Ray Bradbury (1953): Set in a future where books are banned, this novel explores a society controlled by a manipulative government that seeks to suppress knowledge and independent thinking.

"The Handmaid's Tale" by Margaret Atwood (1985): Set in a dystopian society called Gilead, this novel depicts a totalitarian regime that subjugates women for reproductive purposes and controls the population through strict religious rules.

"The Circle" by Dave Eggers (2013): The book follows a young woman who joins a powerful tech company that aims to create a totalitarian surveillance state, blurring the boundaries between privacy and transparency.

"Red Rising" by Pierce Brown (2014): The first book in a science fiction series portrays a futuristic society divided into colour-coded social classes, with the powerful elite exploiting and controlling the lower classes.

Films:

"The Matrix" (1999): Set in a future where humanity is unknowingly trapped in a simulated reality created by machines, the film explores themes of control, manipulation, and the struggle for freedom.

"V for Vendetta" (2005): Adapted from Alan Moore's graphic novel, this film follows a vigilante named V who fights against a fascist regime that manipulates and suppresses the population.

"The Hunger Games" series (2012-2015): Based on Suzanne Collins' novels, these films depict a dystopian society where the ruling elite maintains control through an annual televised event in which young people fight to the death.

"Snowpiercer" (2013): Set aboard a perpetually moving train after a global catastrophe, the film explores social class divisions and control as the elites reside in luxury at the front of the train, while the oppressed lower classes struggle at the tail end.

These are just a few examples, and there are many other films and books that explore similar themes of powerful elites controlling the mass population in various ways.

This and You

If we accept these accepted thoughts, then we see that we live in a social system that is controlled by the elite. Living in a social system that is controlled by the elite can have significant impacts on the way a person thinks and lives each day.

While individuals' experiences may vary, renowned thinkers have explored the consequences of such systems on thought processes, emotions, and overall wellbeing.

Here are some insights from thinkers regarding the effects of self-serving governments and politicians:

- Alienation and Powerlessness: Philosopher Karl Marx discussed how living under a system controlled by the elite can lead to feelings of alienation and powerlessness among the working class. He argued that the exploitative nature of capitalism can result in individuals feeling disconnected from their work, their fellow human beings, and even themselves.

- Manipulation and Manufactured Consent: Noam Chomsky and Edward S. Herman introduced the concept of "manufacturing consent" to describe how the media, which is often influenced by powerful interests, can shape public opinion and support the agendas of the elite. They argued that this manipulation of information can lead individuals to adopt certain beliefs and perspectives that align with the interests of the ruling class.

- Frustration and Despair: Philosopher Jean-Paul Sartre discussed the concept of "bad faith," wherein individuals become trapped in societal expectations and accept the status quo without critically questioning it. Sartre argued that this conformity can lead to a sense of frustration and despair as individuals feel powerless to effect meaningful change.

- Apathy and Disengagement: Political scientist Sheldon Wolin coined the term "inverted totalitarianism" to describe a system where the appearance of democracy is maintained, but power is increasingly concentrated in the hands of a few. Wolin argued that this system can breed apathy and disengagement among citizens, as they feel their voices and actions have little impact on the decisions being made.

- Emotional Toll and Mental Health: While not specific to renowned thinkers, it is worth noting that living in a system that prioritises the interests of the elite over the wellbeing of the general population can have profound effects on individuals' mood and emotions. The erosion of social safety nets, widening inequality, and disregard for social justice can contribute to feelings of anxiety, frustration, and despair among those who are adversely affected.

Michel Foucault: Foucault, a French philosopher and social theorist, explored the relationship between power and knowledge. He argued that power operates through various institutional and discursive mechanisms, shaping individuals' subjectivities and governing their behaviour. His work highlights how living under systems of power can influence individuals' thoughts, actions, and identities.

Paulo Freire: Freire, a Brazilian educator and philosopher, focused on the concept of "oppression" and its effects on individuals and communities. He discussed how oppressive systems, often perpetuated by the elite, dehumanise people and limit their critical thinking. Freire emphasised the importance of critical consciousness and collective action in challenging oppressive structures.

Bell hooks: hooks, an American author and feminist theorist, explored the intersections of race, gender, and class within systems of power. She examined how dominant ideologies and structures of power can shape individuals' perceptions of themselves and others. hooks highlighted the importance of critical thinking and cultural transformation to challenge oppressive systems.

Erich Fromm: Fromm, a social psychologist and philosopher, examined the effects of alienation and the pursuit of material wealth on individuals' wellbeing. He critiqued the influence of consumer culture and capitalism, arguing that they can lead to a sense of emptiness and a lack of authentic human connection. Fromm talked about the importance of cultivating genuine relationships and pursuing self-actualisation.

That's Interesting

Let's look more at Fromm's ideas and conclusions:

- Alienation: Fromm examined the concept of alienation, referring to the feeling of being disconnected from oneself, others, and the world. He argued that modern industrialised societies, driven by capitalist systems, can foster a sense of alienation as individuals become increasingly detached from meaningful human connections and engaged in superficial pursuits.

- Materialism and Consumer Culture: Fromm critiqued the prevailing culture of materialism, where individuals are encouraged to seek fulfilment through the acquisition of goods and possessions. He argued that the pursuit of material wealth alone cannot provide genuine happiness or address the deeper needs and desires of human beings.

- Authentic Human Connection: Fromm pointed out the importance of authentic relationships as a source of fulfilment and wellbeing. He believed that genuine connections with others, based on love, empathy, and mutual understanding, are essential for human flourishing. Fromm highlighted the need for individuals to engage in active dialogue and to overcome the barriers that prevent authentic human connection.

- Critique of Capitalism: Fromm offered a critique of capitalism, asserting that it often prioritises profit and the pursuit of wealth over human wellbeing. He questioned the inherent values and structures of capitalist societies, suggesting that alternative economic systems should be explored to foster greater social harmony, equality, and individual fulfilment.

Evaluating These Thoughts and Texts

The notable aspect of all of this is that writing - through human history and today - is mainly done by people who are good (I say 'all' but let's say 99%+). The people who say things that are about negativity, division, fear and stress now do this through TV news channels and social media.

People already realised - thousands of years ago when we were little more than cave people who lived in outside dwellings and knew how to farm - how we can live well.

Modern writers, in their hundreds, tell us that we are essentially being controlled by people who only want everything to be as they personally want it to be. The powerful people (let's just say men) who hoard enormous wealth and continue to make the world a worse place for the deprived and under-privileged; these men are not writing books on how to do those things.

Of course that sounds obvious, but it's interesting. This book is not about this specific topic and so I will stop short of going further into how we can create a utopia for humanity (as if I have the answer). Yet, the context must be fully seen with harsh and absolute clarity if you are going to fully realise the person who is the most you.

Now this is not advocating that 'the most you' doesn't own possessions. The very real conclusion may be that we could all pretty much find satisfaction if we agree, as one, that we will become monk-like people who simply have self-built shelter and farm crops, but it doesn't seem possible to achieve that.

It's also a bit boring. A bit 'OK, what next?'.

How can you be in control of your mind in a conflicted and controlling world?

Method One: Use Mantras

The concept of mantras originated in ancient Hindu and Buddhist traditions. Mantras are sacred sounds, words, or phrases that are repeated during meditation or as part of spiritual practices. The exact origin of mantras is difficult to pinpoint, as they have evolved and been used across different cultures and time periods.

In Hinduism, the use of mantras can be traced back to the ancient Vedas, the collection of scriptures dating back thousands of years. The Vedas contain hymns and chants that were recited for various purposes, including spiritual upliftment and invoking divine energy. Mantras were seen as a means to connect with higher consciousness and attain spiritual transformation.

In Buddhism, mantras are an integral part of meditation and spiritual practices. The most well-known Buddhist mantra is "Om Mani Padme Hum," which is associated with the bodhisattva of compassion, Avalokiteshvara. This mantra is widely recited by Buddhists as a means to cultivate compassion and wisdom.

The practice of using mantras spread beyond the boundaries of Hinduism and Buddhism. It has been adopted in various forms by different cultures and religions, including Jainism, Sikhism, and certain indigenous traditions.

In Western history, the recognition and exploration of mantras as a therapeutic tool are relatively recent. Again, this doesn't mean that they didn't occur, but our old friends the Druids didn't feel the need to write down their particular words of choice for when they built Stonehenge and faced any challenges along the way.

One key figure in introducing mantras into Western psychological lexicon is the Swiss psychiatrist Carl Jung. He recognized the significance of repetitive sounds and words as a way to access the unconscious mind and facilitate psychological healing. Jung explored the use of mantras and repetitive prayers in his own therapeutic work. He explored the power of repetitive sounds and words in his work, his focus was primarily on the exploration of the unconscious mind and the process of individuation.

Jung's interest in the unconscious and its symbols led him to study various cultural and spiritual traditions, including Eastern philosophies. He recognized the value of practices such as meditation and contemplation in accessing the deeper layers of the psyche. However, it's important to note that Jung's emphasis was more on the psychological and symbolic significance of these practices rather than their specific use as mantras.

Jung's exposure to Eastern philosophies and practices came through his interactions with individuals and texts that brought these ideas to his attention. He incorporated elements from these traditions into his own analytical psychology framework, recognizing their potential for personal growth and transformation.

While Jung did not discover mantras per se, his exploration of symbolism, archetypes, and the power of repetitive practices influenced the integration of Eastern concepts into Western psychological history. He played a significant role in bridging the gap between Western psychology and Eastern traditions, contributing to the broader recognition and adoption of practices like mantras in therapeutic and self-help contexts.

This was developed with the rise of the humanistic and transpersonal psychology movements. Psychologists such as Abraham Maslow, Stanislav Grof, and Ken Wilber incorporated elements of these practices into their theories and therapeutic approaches.

Today, mantras are utilised in various forms of therapy and self-help practices, such as mindfulness-based interventions, cognitive-behavioural therapy, and positive affirmations. They are recognized for their potential to promote focus, relaxation, and emotional wellbeing.

The power of mantras lies in their potential to influence the human brain and facilitate various psychological and physiological effects. From a scientific and neurological perspective, mantras can have a measurable impact on brain activity and functioning. Here's a breakdown of how mantras relate to the human brain:

1. Attention and Focus: Reciting or repeating a mantra engages the brain's attentional networks. It helps redirect attention away from distracting thoughts or external stimuli and focuses it on the present

moment. This process activates the prefrontal cortex, a region involved in attentional control, decision-making, and self-regulation.

2. Neural Pathways and Plasticity: Repetition of a mantra can establish new neural pathways in the brain, a phenomenon known as neuroplasticity. By consistently repeating a specific phrase or sound, the corresponding neural connections strengthen, enhancing the brain's ability to process and integrate that particular information. This can lead to long-term changes in neural activity and structure.

3. Calming the Mind and Reducing Stress: Mantras have been shown to activate the parasympathetic nervous system, which promotes relaxation and counteracts the body's stress response. Research suggests that reciting mantras can lower heart rate, blood pressure, and cortisol levels, providing a sense of calm and reducing stress and anxiety.

4. Mantras and Neural Oscillations: Mantra repetition can synchronise neural oscillations in the brain. Studies using electroencephalography (EEG) have demonstrated that chanting mantras or engaging in rhythmic vocalisations can induce coherent brainwave patterns, such as increased alpha and theta activity. These brainwave states are associated with relaxation, creativity, and enhanced cognitive processing.

5. Emotional Regulation and wellbeing: Mantras have the potential to modulate emotional states by influencing brain regions involved in emotional processing, such as the amygdala and the prefrontal cortex. Regular practice of mantras has been linked to improved emotional regulation, increased positive affect, and reduced symptoms of depression and anxiety.

What's interesting is that something old was adapted into a therapy context.

It raises the question that there was a period of time in which they weren't needed. Of course, the idea of medicine, healing, therapy and the like have only improved over time. This is obvious, because as time goes on, humans know more and, generally, life gets better for more people. Let's say if we compare any time in the last thousand years to how people live now, and, we can generally agree that the general population lives better off.

However, although people can live well, it's not all milk and honey. The pros and cons are easy to see, as modern life brings different types of pressures and challenges.

So although someone with, let's say, 'mental problems' may have been taken away or dunked under water hundreds of years ago, many people did live well.

If you were in a small English village in the 1800s, then live could have consisted of rising and sleeping with the pattern of the Sun, eating only seasonal, locally produced vegetables, connecting with family members and the local community, caring not for material possessions, not having ANY screen time, not sitting in traffic, not being told fear-mongering news.

There are concepts of solutions or therapies to cure or overcome, but if prevention is better, then we have to look at what we can take from pre-modern lifestyles in order to live well.

One thing in particular that they didn't have was relentless instant access to other people's thoughts and fears.

Method Two: Understand how media works

Social media has always existed, if you consider that a notice in a Town Square hundreds of years ago was both social and a form of media. The difference is the quantity or frequency that we can now choose to receive it. But, it's also more than that. The difference is that now is the most consumerist time of humanity's existence.

This means that people are keen to show off the stuff they have, but also, it means that money can be made from traditional media.

It is helpful to see all media as business, not an information source. They are profit-driven entities. Of course, they each would say that they have editorial standards, integrity and credibility. You wouldn't expect them to say that they don't have these things, would you?

This is from a BBC article:

They are talking about the possibility of the London Mayor Sadiq Khan resisting a possible lockdown for London.

The Department of Health adviser suggests: "Rather than doing too much forward signalling, we can roll pitch with the new strain."

Mr Hancock says: "We frighten the pants of everyone with the new strain."

The adviser responds: "Yep, that's what will get proper behaviour change."

The minister then asks: "When do we deploy the new variant."

Mr Hancock announced the new variant the following day.

This is from an article in The Independent:

Meanwhile, Mr Sunak is under pressure to answer questions about whether Treasury officials ignored evidence that his summer 2020 Eat Out to Help Out scheme helped spread the virus.

On 24 August 2020, Mr Hancock told Mr Case he had "kept it out of the news" in a message suggesting that the scheme boosting the economy had had a negative impact in terms of infections.

He said: "We have had lots of feedback that [Eat Out to Help Out] is causing problems... I've kept it out of the news but it's serious. So please please let's not allow the economic success of the scheme to lead to its extension."

This could lead a sane person to believe that government politicians control what the public see in the news.

I attempted to research the issue of how much of what you see in the news is placed there by agencies, but to little surprise, this is never declared. So, I can only share anecdotally with you from the time I worked within the magazine/media world, separately in the PR world and when I knew people in PR.

Anecdotally, the conclusion is 'much' of what you see in the news has been placed there. You would be surprised on the range and scale of different 'interests' that pay PR agencies. It's not just companies looking to sell their product or service, but it's individuals and organisations. Importantly, PR is there when you don't even know it. Here's one simple example: there was an article about a female racing driver in a tabloid European newspaper. It was a standard interview in which she talked about her experiences. The photo for the article - taking up most of the page - was a shot of a Formula 1 race in Monaco. Now, in the background of the photo you happened to see the advertising hoarding that runs round the race tracks of Formula 1 races. The company that you could see (it was an investment and trading company) on the advertising boards was the company that paid an agency to creatively get them subliminal coverage in the media. You might read an article about a figure of the British Royal family, and somewhere in the controversial piece will be a line that 'Meghan was wearing platinum', and it was paid for by the group that platinum jewellers pay to promote the metal. And, there are just obvious articles in which the journalist innocently 'reviews' a new mobile phone or a video game, but is paid to do so (either outright or in gifts).

The funny thing is, even if you know this, it's easy to gloss over the impact it has on the whole, the most you.

If we break it down into the following areas, then we can look at it through a lens of not YOU, but other people. Why? Because YOU are in a world of others, and their brain occurrences and beliefs and behaviours will likely affect yours:

Doom scrolling refers to the act of continuously scrolling through negative or distressing news and social media content, even when it has a negative impact on one's wellbeing. The reasons behind doom scrolling and the appeal of negative news can be attributed to several factors:

Negativity Bias: The human brain has a natural inclination towards paying more attention to negative stimuli. This bias evolved as a survival mechanism to help us quickly identify potential threats in our environment. Negative news triggers this bias, capturing our attention and evoking emotional responses.

Fear and Anxiety: Negative news often stimulates feelings of fear and anxiety. These emotions activate the amygdala, the brain's emotional centre, which can lead to heightened alertness and attention. People may continue to engage with negative news as a way to stay informed about potential threats and dangers in their environment.

Social and Emotional Connection: Negative news can elicit strong emotional reactions, and people may seek out such content to feel a sense of emotional connection. Sharing and discussing negative news with others can create a sense of camaraderie and validation, reinforcing social bonds.

Cognitive Dissonance: Some individuals may be drawn to negative news due to cognitive dissonance, which is the discomfort experienced when one's beliefs or values conflict with the information they encounter. Engaging with negative news can validate pre-existing beliefs or reinforce biases, reducing cognitive dissonance.

Sensationalism and Media Influence: News outlets often rely on sensationalism and dramatic storytelling to capture audience attention and boost ratings. The media's focus on negative or divisive stories can create a sense of urgency and intrigue, leading people to continue consuming such content.

If you were to simply suggest, to someone you know, that either the news they see is controlled, or that their thoughts, beliefs and emotions are controlled in the same way, they would likely disagree. Most people need the concepts of stability and trust in authority. Most people believe that they are not stupid enough to be fooled.

Now, the simplest way to avoid this particular aspect is to question everything you see in the news. The difficulty can lie in telling other people this, because they may feel as though you are saying that you are more intelligent than they are.

Method Three: Just Stop Sugar

In the olden days, as we glamourise their innocence and nature a little, they didn't have processed food and so much sugar.

Refined sugar isn't great for you and it's better for you to eat fruit and salad. I am sure that you accept this, but much like the news and media angle, sugar isn't just slightly bad for you. It's life-changingly bad for you, so you might want to have less or none.

Refined sugar can destroy the potential power of your brain process, brain quality, acuity, functioning and wellness, in all ways.

Here's some science on it if you are into that kind of thing:

Impaired memory and learning are significant cognitive impairments associated with excessive sugar intake. Synaptic plasticity, the brain's ability to form and strengthen connections between neurons, plays a crucial role in memory formation and learning.

High-sugar diets have been shown to negatively impact synaptic plasticity, which can contribute to memory deficits.

Several studies have examined the effects of sugar on synaptic plasticity and memory in animal models, providing insights into the underlying mechanisms. For instance, a study conducted by Molteni et al. (2002) investigated the impact of a high-sugar diet on spatial learning and memory in rats. The rats were divided into two groups: one group received a high-sugar diet, while the other group received a standard diet. The results showed that the rats on the high-sugar diet exhibited impaired performance in spatial memory tasks compared to those on the standard diet. Additionally, the high-sugar diet group showed decreased synaptic plasticity in the hippocampus, a brain region crucial for memory formation.

Further research by Ross et al. (2009) explored the effects of high-fructose corn syrup (HFCS), a common sweetener in processed foods, on synaptic plasticity in the hippocampus. The study used an animal model and found that long-term consumption of HFCS impaired synaptic plasticity in the hippocampus, leading to deficits in spatial learning and memory.

These studies highlight the detrimental effects of excessive sugar intake on synaptic plasticity and memory formation. But how does sugar impact synaptic plasticity? One key mechanism involves the disruption of insulin signalling in the brain.

Insulin plays a vital role in regulating glucose metabolism, but it also acts as a signalling molecule in the brain, modulating synaptic plasticity and memory processes.

Animal studies have shown that high sugar diets can lead to insulin resistance in the brain, impairing its ability to respond to insulin signals effectively.

This disruption in insulin signalling can interfere with the molecular pathways involved in synaptic plasticity, such as the activation of the protein kinase B (Akt)/mammalian target of rapamycin (mTOR) pathway, which is critical for synaptic growth and strengthening.

Furthermore, excessive sugar intake can also contribute to inflammation and oxidative stress in the brain, which further impairs synaptic plasticity.

Inflammation and oxidative stress disrupt the balance of neurotransmitters, promote the release of pro-inflammatory molecules, and damage neurons, ultimately affecting synaptic plasticity and memory.

While the aforementioned studies primarily focus on animal models, it is important to note that human studies have also shown associations between high sugar intake and cognitive impairments.

A longitudinal study by Crichton et al. (2012) found that higher sugar consumption was associated with poorer cognitive performance and reduced memory in older adults.

In summary, excessive sugar intake can impair memory and learning through its negative impact on synaptic plasticity.

Chronic consumption of high-sugar diets can indeed promote inflammation and oxidative stress in the brain, both of which can have detrimental effects on cognitive function.

Oxidative stress can damage brain cells and contribute to cognitive decline. It can lead to the impairment of neuronal structure and function, including synaptic dysfunction and neuronal death. These changes can have a profound impact on cognitive processes, including memory, attention, and decision-making.

The relationship between the psychology of self-identity, success in life, and the effects of sugar on inflammation and oxidative stress is complex and multifaceted. While there is limited research directly linking these factors, there are some indirect connections worth considering.

Impairments in cognitive function, such as memory deficits or decreased attention span, can hinder an individual's ability to perform tasks effectively, make decisions, and pursue their goals.

Moreover, inflammation and oxidative stress have been linked to mood disorders, such as depression and anxiety, which can impact an individual's self-identity and overall wellbeing.

Weaning oneself off of sugar can be a gradual process that requires commitment and persistence. Stress can trigger sugar cravings for some individuals. Recognise any moments these cravings arise and have a prepared alternative solution.

If the cravings reach a peak, then get busy in some sense. If you can, distract yourself with anything such as exercise or something at home. Get your mouth 'busy' with fruit, nuts and a large glass of water. Fill yourself up with anything healthy as a better alternative to processed junk.

Focusing this much on sugar in 'how to be the most you' might seem like a boring plot twist but it's effective and real.

So the question is, for someone who has invested quite some time into reading about how to be the most you, are you willing to take the road to a (very mainly) sugar-free life?

Method Four: Mature Acceptance of the Machine

Young people around 17 to 23 learn new things about the world that they didn't previously know. They have a natural inclination against these things, either because these things that they discover are disagreeable and unjust, or possibly because that stage of age comes with innate rebelliousness and urges to make changes. Probably the first one.

This isn't a generalisation. First-hand being of that age tells me that when I Was that age, that was the type of discussion had. It's also an accepted stereotype. Stereotypes are OK if we accept that the mass majority of examples are true.

The negative part of stereotypes is if they are ONLY accepted but then nothing happens next, if it needs to.

Young people have certain luxuries such as (usually) few responsibilities. Of course, a young person could possibly say that the world they live in today has been ruined by 'boomers' and therefore they have lots of worries and pressure and so on. This is OK if they disagree - because they are just being their true - or most - selves: young and rebellious.

Yet, they do in fact have less responsibilities if they are not specifically 'caring' (in real terms) for another human, such as a child or other person who needs care.

The problem is that society then decides that they need to get careers and learn and succeed (and fail too, but definitely do succeed somewhere along the line) and then find love, love and be loved, have kids and then sacrifice lots of personal pleasure in order to raise those kids.

And thus the energetic rebelliousness of youth becomes more concerned with lots of other day-to-day things.

This is not only understandable, but also difficult to simply recommend against.

It's an older discussion - say, around the 2000s area - about why people should or shouldn't or do or don't have kids. People without children would feel the need to 'explain' why they don't have children (and in many smaller social circles the contention still exists today, of course).

What's becoming more socially understood these days, is that some people do have kids and some don't. There will of course be cases of any break from the norm being difficult to accept by some people. That's unavoidable.

The point here is that therefore not (at all) that people 'should' have kids, but, for most humans, this will be something that they either aspire to or just do out of nature and/or social nurture.

As well as being a wonderful part of life (in many people's opinions), it also gives you something to lose, figuratively. This lowers people's ambitions and also their will to expend energy for the greater good. They are less willing to take risks.

And it's very risky to try and upset the apple cart of the mega rich.

Here are twenty famous examples of individuals who died, either assassinated or under mysterious circumstances, after attempting to change the status quo of society and enact significant changes:

Martin Luther King Jr. (1929-1968) - Assassinated civil rights leader who fought against racial discrimination and advocated for equality and justice.

John F. Kennedy (1917-1963) - Assassinated U.S. President who aimed to bring about various social and political reforms during his presidency.

Mahatma Gandhi (1869-1948) - Prominent leader of India's independence movement who championed nonviolent resistance and social justice. He was assassinated by a Hindu nationalist.

Malcolm X (1925-1965) - Activist and prominent figure in the Civil Rights Movement who advocated for black empowerment. He was assassinated by members of the Nation of Islam.

Abraham Lincoln (1809-1865) - Assassinated U.S. President who led the country through the Civil War and played a pivotal role in ending slavery.

Olof Palme (1927-1986) - Swedish Prime Minister who pursued progressive social policies and was assassinated in a street shooting.

Patrice Lumumba (1925-1961) - Congolese independence leader and the first Prime Minister of the Democratic Republic of Congo. He was assassinated under disputed circumstances.

Thomas Sankara (1949-1987) - Former President of Burkina Faso who sought to bring about social and political change through his progressive policies. He was assassinated in a coup.

Benazir Bhutto (1953-2007) - Former Prime Minister of Pakistan, Bhutto campaigned for democracy and women's rights. She was assassinated in a suicide attack.

Salvador Allende (1908-1973) - Chilean President who pursued socialist policies and was overthrown in a military coup. He died during the coup.

Steve Biko (1946-1977) - Anti-apartheid activist in South Africa who fought against racial segregation and died while in police custody.

Che Guevara (1928-1967) - Argentine Marxist revolutionary who played a significant role in the Cuban Revolution. He was captured and executed in Bolivia.

Indira Gandhi (1917-1984) - Former Prime Minister of India who implemented significant policies but was assassinated by her bodyguards.

Anna Politkovskaya (1958-2006) - Russian investigative journalist and human rights activist known for her critical reporting on the Russian government. She was assassinated.

Fred Hampton (1948-1969) - American civil rights activist and leader of the Black Panther Party. He was killed in a raid conducted by the FBI and Chicago police.

Pier Paolo Pasolini (1922-1975) - Italian filmmaker, writer, and intellectual who challenged societal norms through his works. He was murdered under mysterious circumstances.

Medgar Evers (1925-1963) - Civil rights activist who fought against segregation in the United States. He was assassinated by a white supremacist.

Jo Cox (1974-2016) - British Member of Parliament known for her advocacy on humanitarian issues. She was assassinated by a far-right extremist.

Daphne Caruana Galizia (1964-2017) - Maltese investigative journalist known for her exposés on corruption. She was killed in a car bomb explosion.

Berta Cáceres (1971-2016) - Honduran environmental activist who fought against the construction of a hydroelectric dam. She was assassinated for her activism.

Do you see? Well, just in case, here are a further twenty:

Anna Mae Aquash (1945-1975) - American First Nations activist who fought for Native American rights and was involved in the American Indian Movement. She was murdered.

Walter Rodney (1942-1980) - Guyanese historian, activist, and Marxist scholar who advocated for decolonization and social justice. He was assassinated in Guyana.

Rachel Corrie (1979-2003) - American activist who protested against the Israeli occupation of Palestine. She was killed by an Israeli military bulldozer in Gaza.

Marielle Franco (1979-2018) - Brazilian politician, feminist, and human rights activist who advocated for marginalised communities. She was assassinated in Rio de Janeiro.

Jamal Khashoggi (1958-2018) - Saudi Arabian journalist and dissident who was critical of the Saudi government. He was assassinated inside the Saudi consulate in Istanbul.

Chico Mendes (1944-1988) - Brazilian environmentalist and trade union leader who fought against deforestation and land exploitation in the Amazon rainforest. He was assassinated.

Ken Saro-Wiwa (1941-1995) - Nigerian writer and environmental activist who opposed the activities of multinational oil companies in the Niger Delta. He was executed by the Nigerian government.

Berta Cáceres (1971-2016) - Honduran environmental and indigenous rights activist who opposed the construction of a dam. She was assassinated in her home.

Chokri Belaid (1964-2013) - Tunisian politician and human rights advocate who criticized the government. He was assassinated in Tunis.

Natalya Estemirova (1958-2009) - Russian human rights activist who exposed abuses in Chechnya. She was kidnapped and murdered.

Benazir Bhutto (1953-2007) - Former Prime Minister of Pakistan and prominent political figure who campaigned for democracy. She was assassinated in a suicide attack.

Boris Nemtsov (1959-2015) - Russian opposition politician who spoke out against Vladimir Putin's government. He was shot and killed in Moscow.

Hrant Dink (1954-2007) - Turkish-Armenian journalist and editor who advocated for recognition of the Armenian Genocide. He was assassinated in Istanbul.

Alexander Litvinenko (1962-2006) - Russian dissident and former FSB officer who accused the Russian government of corruption. He was poisoned with polonium-210 in London.

U Ko Ni (1953-2017) - Burmese lawyer and advocate for democracy and human rights. He was assassinated at an airport in Myanmar.

Sergei Yushenkov (1950-2003) - Russian politician and critic of the Russian government. He was assassinated outside his home in Moscow.

Zoran Djindjic (1952-2003) - Serbian Prime Minister who sought to reform the country and bring about democracy. He was assassinated in Belgrade.

Sabeen Mahmud (1974-2015) - Pakistani human rights activist and founder of a social forum promoting free speech and critical dialogue. She was killed in a targeted attack in Karachi.

Lasantha Wickrematunge (1958-2009) - Sri Lankan journalist and editor who exposed government corruption and human rights abuses. He was assassinated in Colombo.

Kem Ley (1970-2016) - Cambodian political analyst and critic of the government. He was shot and killed in Phnom Penh.

Above is the drop in the ocean, the famous cases that sometimes happened in supposedly nations with a free press, if there is such a thing. There is no way to research and list all people who suffered similar fates after trying to enact change in countries where such consequences are everyday and commonplace.

This is relevant to 'being the most YOU' as we come back to the stated 'method four: mature acceptance'.

I am absolutely not advocating that anyone should advocate for change. It would be hypocritical and immature and irresponsible to do that because it would be advocating risk. Which is not what this is about.

This book is not about 'how we can make the world a better place'. There must be other books about that. Creating utopia is a lovely dream but may not be possible.

This is about how you can realistically feel able to reach, enact, enable and enjoy the qualities that you see as your 'most good', that you like, or even love.

With an accepted context of your mind being manipulated for the financial gain of complete strangers (who are already billionaires), this can assist in the unencumbered vivacity of your mind.

It doesn't mean that we need to regress to immaturity; the immature belief being held in the context of having apparently deep discussions with other people aged 17-23 about how wrong the world is. It's not about angst nor hand wringing nor Champagne socialism nor virtue signalling.

Mature acceptance is contextual to living real life, not to glamourising martyrs.

Mature acceptance doesn't mean watching wild theories on Instagram - or even logical ones.

Russell Brand has an Instagram account on which he speaks a lot about those with lots of power doing lots of controlling things in order to get more power and money. That's roughly how he speaks too, so I think that's fair. Anyway, what he then does is do things like sell tickets to go and watch him talk about these things on stage.

After watching his words - either on their phone or in the theatre - what changes do you think the audience members make; if any? Or do they make no changes and just watch him perform and then leave the theatre, drive their car home, take off their made-in-somewhere-foreign clothes, put down their human-slave-made phone and then buy things the next day?

There is no obvious way to live in our current world that doesn't somehow make you part of the system.

So if you're a late teen listening to Rage Against The Machine on your device and thinking 'yeah man I was born to rage against 'em too man', or a grown adult watching Russell Brand et al opine on unfairness but then still basically going along with it, then beware that those two actors are also still part of the system. More accurate would be Rage Against The Machine But Then Still Just Go Along With It Because You Need Clothes And Transport.

THUS: You don't need to feel guilty - you just need to be aware of the current state of things and then feel comfortable in your level of reaction. This could be donating clothes or it could be thinking 'fuck it I am not going to really enact greatly positive environmental change in my lifetime so I am just going to live well'. Even if you thought that last one, you wouldn't really be doing more environmental damage than someone who felt anxiety every time they mentioned something related on the 'news'.

It may still smart, it may still feel frustrating to accept that 'the news' is simply the fear-mongering clickbait of the day - and most of society unquestioningly laps it up - but at least the acceptance means you can mentally function without taking the bait of fear yourself. You can feel psychologically removed from the noise and look in as something of an outsider. That way, you are looking at it, seeing it, taking it in, as you. Not 'a reader' or 'a consumer' or even a stakeholder or affected party. You retain the mental you-ness of each day without being essentially mindfucked by the elite or Russell Brand.

Method Five: Be as mindful as you want

As we have seen, unless you skipped the educational bits, accepted theories of mental creaminess fulcrumise themselves around mindfulness, introspection, meditation. Thinking and that.

Going against the grain

In techniques of doing wellbeing, mindfulness is mentioned. Mindfulness is simple and good. It's basically awareness, one of the important traits that we've already discussed.

Mindfulness is another way of saying stop and think about what you are doing. Actions have consequences, so what are the consequences of your actions in life? Just like kids are told to count to 10 before replying if they feel angry, mindfulness means noticing what is happening rather than letting it pass by. Pause for a moment before taking actions.

This is great, but anything can go too far. For the concerned amongst us, being too mindful, too aware, too questioning, can lead us to go round in circles. Hence the timeless phrase 'too much of a good thing'. Old phrases last generations because they are very accurate.

Mindless living can also be good. Look, I've listed a few reasons why!

37

Mindless eating

What would tantalise me? Thrill me? What would really set the tone for current life? What are people eating/photographing on social media? These are questions that can drive your relationship with food toward fat, sugar and stress.

Picking 'just the right' restaurant that will thrill your life and really let people know on social media that you are living it right up is also too much hard work. People who do not feel anxiety may find this bizarre. How can we let something as simple as eating cause us angst? Because we are special.

I have found it helpful to simplify eating. Not always, sometimes just on weekdays, or for periods of time. Quickly frying/roasting/steaming 'some sliced vegetables' and 'some protein' and a carbohydrate with some herbs and then adding a couple of favourite condiments is a very healthy, filling and stress-free way to enjoy a meal without any emotional baggage attached.

I don't eat it 'mindfully', thinking about each grain of brown rice. Safe in the knowledge that it's healthy and filling, my mind can drift into a subconscious flow state.

Mindless weekending

Watching TV and going for a walk and doing mindless eating and tidying the house is a great way to spend a weekend. And when colleagues or anyone asks "how was your weekend", don't say you did nothing, say it was "great!". It is great to not have the hassle of creating unforgettable memories or precious, rosy-cheeked times just because it's a Saturday and Sunday. Don't even say you 'binge watched' something, because that's still some kind of pseudo-cool tick-box that causes people to unnecessarily reference Netflix. Use mindless, non-socially approved wording and enjoy the power of individuality.

Mindless parenting

Tired parenting can be better. You know the moment where the other parent contradicts what you've said to your kid – in front of the kid? And you get all ego-fueled and uppity that your parenting word has not been seen as sacred? That usually happens with the first child. By the time you're in the baby years of the second, you lack the energy or spirit to care that your golden word has been muddied. You are too tired to care. This is great because you won't start a meaningless argument with your spouse, you'll just lightly shrug your shoulders and go back to munching your steamed vegetables.

Mindless working

If you are doing things and then people pay you to do those things, then it's a wonderful mindless win. While others are keenly posting about their new job or award or recent project that their employer did – don't. As they are 'excited to be a part of' and 'delighted to announce' and commenting that there's a 'great line up' for the next webinar (or Hybrid Forum, Symposium etc) and virtue signalling the life out of whatever is trending that day and that day alone, quietly think to yourself that you are greatly enjoying the money that your job has provided.

If others race to sign up to the 'work thing that's not a work thing but will score you points with management', then do your contracted tasks really really well but don't stress about bottom-licking endeavours. This also comes back to setting out your stall, as mentioned previously.

Mindless living

Maybe go for a run, maybe don't. Maybe choose a roasted vegetable dinner, maybe have noodles. If another driver over-takes, swerves in front of you or does something idiotic, don't put your foot down or compete with them for nothing. If a friend or family member talks politics then politely nod along. These inactions mean that when the moment stops, you don't have any left-over second-thoughts, angst, regrets or emotional stickiness. We'll talk about inaction in the next section.

Mind-body connection

Mindfulness suggests that you need to sit and think deeply. Don't! Move your body instead.

How can mindlessly moving your body transform your mind?

1. Increased Blood Flow: Walking stimulates blood circulation throughout the body, including the brain. This increased blood flow delivers a fresh supply of oxygen and vital nutrients to the brain cells, supporting their optimal function. Adequate oxygenation and nutrient supply are crucial for maintaining the energy levels required for efficient thinking and information processing.

2. Neurogenesis and Brain Plasticity: Walking has been shown to promote neurogenesis, which is the generation of new neurons (brain cells) in certain regions of the brain. It particularly affects the hippocampus, a region involved in memory and learning. Neurogenesis is associated with improved cognitive function, better memory formation, and enhanced ability to acquire new skills. Additionally, walking also supports brain plasticity, the brain's ability to adapt and reorganise its structure in response to experiences and learning.

3. Neurotransmitter Release: Walking triggers the release of various neurotransmitters, chemicals that facilitate communication between brain cells. One such neurotransmitter is dopamine, which is involved in reward, motivation, and attention. Increased dopamine release during walking can improve focus and concentration, leading to better cognitive performance. Additionally, walking also promotes the release of endorphins, serotonin, and norepinephrine,

which contribute to mood regulation and a sense of wellbeing.

4. Stress Reduction: Walking serves as a form of physical exercise that can alleviate stress and anxiety. Exercise has been shown to decrease levels of cortisol, a stress hormone that can impair cognitive function when present in excess. By reducing stress, walking helps create a conducive environment for clear thinking and problem-solving.

5. Enhanced Brain Connectivity: Walking has been associated with improved connectivity between different brain regions. It promotes the formation and strengthening of neural pathways, enabling efficient communication between various cognitive processes. This increased connectivity can enhance overall cognitive performance, including memory, attention, and decision-making.

6. Mood Enhancement: Walking in natural environments or green spaces has been linked to improved mood and reduced symptoms of depression. A positive mood state can contribute to better cognitive functioning, creativity, and flexible thinking.

Never think of yourself as beyond science.

You may be feeling stressed, but that doesn't mean that gravity doesn't apply.

Never assume that your physical state is not affecting you.

How can going for a walk directly affect the problem that's making you worry? Maybe it won't, but your mindset is made up of neurons and cells and things. It's not made of stone. It can change. Going for a walk can divert your mind into a more subconscious, less worried status wherein you are able to gain a new perspective, outside of the aforementioned context of control and conflict. Go there, be that.

PART TWO:
YOUR HEART

Your Heart

Love is funny because it is accepted as a good thing - unless you love something too much. Then it can be said to be a bad thing. Or unrequited love, when you love someone that doesn't love you. But is that really love if it's not two-way?

So we have: loving something too much: bad. But you can't really love something 'not enough', because then it means you just don't love it.

So we understand: that there is a tipping point by which it can be declared that we love a thing or person.

But, if you keep going deep into the scale of love, it can go 'too far'!

This nonsensical meandering is all to say that people are and will always be fascinated by love, because it's mysterious and rare, thus it has value.

What then happens is that society, media and people refer to love in order to increase the value of their thing. Film studios can hope to make more money if they trigger certain emotions in the audience. Sex gets wrapped up with love, and therefore you are told to buy many, many things to get love and be loved.

Love is security, and we also want that, so people want to appear lovable, even if they very much are not. Which is how divorce happens.

The General Idea of Love

Love is a complex emotion that is deeply ingrained in human experience. It encompasses a range of feelings, attitudes, and behaviours that connect individuals in profound and meaningful ways.

While it can be challenging to define love definitively, it can be understood through various perspectives and dimensions.

Emotionally, love is often associated with affection, warmth, and attachment towards someone or something. It involves a deep sense of care, empathy, and compassion, where individuals genuinely desire the wellbeing and happiness of the object of their love.

Love can bring about intense feelings of joy, contentment, and fulfilment, while also making individuals vulnerable to pain, heartbreak, and longing.

Love extends beyond emotion and influences our thoughts and actions. It can drive people to make sacrifices, prioritise the needs of others, and engage in selfless acts of kindness.

Romantic love involves passionate and intimate connections between partners, characterised by attraction, desire, and an emotional bond.

Familial love is rooted in the deep bond between family members, shaped by shared experiences, support, and unconditional acceptance. Love between friends is based on mutual affection, trust, and companionship.

Love can be accompanied by jealousy, possessiveness, and conflict.

In summary, love encompasses a rich tapestry of emotions, behaviours, and connections that bring meaning and joy to our lives.

It is a fundamental aspect of human existence that shapes our relationships, fuels personal growth, and fosters a sense of belonging and interconnectedness with others and the world around us.

Self Love

It sounds a bit odd, but we are talking about self love from the emotional side, not the genitalia side. That's what we're looking at here, because wellbeing, self-development and such things usually talk about 'you have to love yourself first'.

Do you? I'm not convinced it goes into the realm of *love*, but, as said above, love is regularly picked as the bait because it's what humans want.

In context, self love can be explained to someone who is actively hurting themselves or doing something that is not healthy or good for them. Yet that feels like a simplification and ignores their motives for the self-harm. Telling a teenager that they shouldn't vape because it's bad for them and they should love themselves instead: this is wishy-washy adult advice and ignores that intense hormonal cravings that peer pressure presents.

Also, as we know, some people are assholes, and they should *not* love themselves.

The Historical Context

The concept of "loving oneself" or practising "self love" is a topic that has been widely explored and debated among psychologists and thinkers. While there is no unanimous consensus on the matter, various perspectives exist regarding the ability to love oneself and its significance in psychological wellbeing.

Many renowned psychologists and thinkers emphasise the importance of self-love as a crucial component of mental and emotional health. They argue that cultivating a positive and compassionate relationship with oneself is essential for overall wellbeing and personal growth. Psychologists such as Carl Rogers and Abraham Maslow have emphasised the significance of self-acceptance and self-esteem in leading fulfilling lives.

Carl Rogers, a prominent humanistic psychologist, highlighted the concept of self-actualization, which involves striving to reach one's full potential. Central to this process is self-acceptance and self-regard, where individuals nurture a positive self-image and treat themselves with kindness and understanding. According to Rogers, self-love is foundational to healthy relationships and personal development.

Abraham Maslow's hierarchy of needs theory also suggests that self-esteem, including self-love, is a fundamental psychological need. Maslow posited that individuals must

46

satisfy their basic needs, including self-esteem and self-respect, before reaching the highest level of self-actualization.

Furthermore, proponents of cognitive-behavioural therapy (CBT) mention the role of self-compassion and self-care in promoting mental wellbeing. CBT encourages individuals to challenge negative self-perceptions, practice self-acceptance, and engage in self-care activities that nurture emotional and physical health.

However, it is important to note that the concept of self-love is not without criticism. Some argue that an excessive focus on self-love or self-esteem can lead to narcissism or an inflated sense of entitlement. Critics claim that true self-esteem should be rooted in genuine personal achievements and character rather than a superficial sense of self-worth.

Additionally, psychologists like Albert Ellis, the founder of rational emotive behaviour therapy (REBT), have argued that self-acceptance is more important than self-love. Ellis believed that individuals should focus on accepting themselves unconditionally, including their flaws and imperfections, rather than striving for self-love, which can be more elusive and potentially harmful if based on external validation.

Different Things That Sound Similar:

Self-love, self-acceptance, and self-esteem are interconnected but distinct concepts within the realm of self-compassion and personal wellbeing. While they share similarities, understanding their differences can provide clarity on how they contribute to a healthy self-perception.

Self-Love: Self-love refers to a deep sense of care, kindness, and compassion towards oneself. It involves nurturing a positive and nurturing relationship with oneself, treating oneself with gentleness and understanding. Self-love entails recognizing one's worth, acknowledging personal strengths, and embracing both the positive and negative aspects of oneself. It involves self care, setting healthy boundaries, and making choices that honour one's wellbeing. Self-love is more about valuing oneself as a whole and recognizing that one's worth is not contingent upon external validation.

Self-Acceptance: Self-acceptance involves embracing and acknowledging oneself as one is, without judgement or the need for change. It is the willingness to recognize and embrace all aspects of oneself, including strengths, weaknesses, flaws, and imperfections. Self-acceptance involves letting go of the pursuit of an idealised version of oneself and embracing authenticity. It is about cultivating a non-judgmental and compassionate attitude towards oneself, recognizing that being human means having both positive and negative traits. Self-acceptance fosters a sense of peace and contentment with oneself, promoting mental wellbeing and reducing self-criticism.

Self-Esteem: Self-esteem refers to the overall evaluation and perception of one's worth and value. It encompasses the beliefs and opinions individuals hold about themselves, including their abilities, accomplishments, and self-perception. Self-esteem can be influenced by internal factors such as self-perception and self-reflection, as well as external factors such as social comparisons and feedback from others. Healthy self-esteem involves having a realistic and balanced view of oneself, recognizing one's strengths while acknowledging areas for growth. It is about valuing oneself and having confidence in one's abilities and worth.

While self-love, self-acceptance, and self-esteem are interconnected, they differ in focus and emphasis.

In practice, cultivating self-love, self-acceptance, and self-esteem can be mutually reinforcing.

When individuals cultivate self-love and self-acceptance, they can develop a more balanced and realistic self-esteem.

Conversely, having healthy self-esteem can contribute to a positive self-perception and the ability to practise self-love and self-acceptance.

Identifying the Self

This is all well and good, if the self is good.

What have people recorded into the annals of psychology about identifying the self?

Self-identity is a complex and multifaceted concept that has been explored by renowned psychologists and authors. While different perspectives exist, many experts recognise the importance of self-reflection, self-awareness, and personal growth in developing a clear and content self-identity.

Here are some insights and suggestions from prominent figures in psychology and literature, let's gooooo:

Carl Rogers:

Rogers, a humanistic psychologist, recognised the significance of congruence or self-consistency in self-identity. He believed that individuals who experience congruence between their self-concept (how they perceive themselves) and their actual experiences are more likely to have a clear and authentic self-identity.

To achieve congruence, Rogers suggested engaging in self-exploration and self-acceptance. This involves being open to experiencing and understanding one's emotions, thoughts, values, and desires without judgement or self-criticism.

Erik Erikson:

Erikson, a developmental psychologist, proposed a theory of psychosocial development that includes the concept of identity formation. According to Erikson, individuals go through various stages of development, and successfully resolving the identity crisis during adolescence leads to a clear and well-defined self-identity.

One exercise inspired by Erikson's theory is the "identity exploration" process, where individuals reflect on their values, interests, talents, and aspirations. They explore different roles, beliefs, and experiences to shape their identity consciously.

Brené Brown:

Brown, a researcher and author, explores the concept of self-identity in the context of vulnerability and wholehearted living. She spoke about the importance of embracing one's imperfections and being authentic in order to develop a genuine sense of self.

One practice Brown suggests is cultivating self-compassion. This involves treating oneself with kindness, understanding, and forgiveness, especially during moments of self-doubt or setbacks. By practising self-compassion, individuals can build a healthier relationship with themselves and enhance their self-identity.

Carl Rogers believed in the transformative power of congruence between one's self-concept and actual experiences.

He wrote about the importance of self-exploration, self-acceptance, and genuine interactions with others to achieve this congruence.

1. Self-Exploration: Rogers believed that self-exploration is a fundamental step toward achieving congruence. To explore oneself, one must engage in honest and non-judgmental introspection.

2. This involves gaining insight into one's emotions, thoughts, values, and desires. Here are some strategies for self-exploration:

3. Reflection: Take the time to reflect on your experiences, both positive and negative. Ask yourself questions about how you felt, what you learned, and how these experiences shape your self-concept.

4. Journaling: Write down your thoughts and feelings regularly. Use your journal as a safe space to express yourself honestly, without fear of judgement. This practice allows for deeper self-awareness and can reveal patterns or themes in your experiences.

5. Mindfulness: Practise being fully present in the moment and observing your thoughts and emotions without judgement. Mindfulness helps you develop a deeper understanding of yourself and enhances your ability to engage authentically with your experiences.

6. Self-Acceptance: Rogers mentioned the importance of self-acceptance as a cornerstone of congruence.

7. Accepting oneself means embracing all aspects of who you are, including your strengths, weaknesses, and vulnerabilities. Here are some strategies for cultivating self-acceptance:

8. Self-Compassion: Treat yourself with kindness, understanding, and forgiveness. Practice self-compassion by offering yourself the same care and support you would give to a close friend facing challenges or setbacks. This compassionate attitude fosters acceptance and reduces self-criticism.

9. Embracing Imperfections: Recognize that being human means having imperfections and making mistakes. Embrace your imperfections as part of your unique self. Instead of striving for perfection, focus on personal growth and learning from your experiences.

10. Letting Go of Judgement: Release the need to judge yourself or compare yourself to others. Appreciate your own journey and acknowledge that everyone has their own unique path. Embracing your individuality allows for greater self-acceptance.

11. Genuine Interactions with Others: Rogers believed that authentic and empathetic interactions with others are

essential for congruence. Genuine relationships provide opportunities for self-discovery and acceptance. Here are some suggestions for fostering genuine interactions:

12. Active Listening: Develop the skill of active listening, where you fully engage with others, seek to understand their perspective, and respond with empathy. This genuine connection deepens mutual understanding and encourages others to reciprocate, creating an environment conducive to personal growth.

13. Non-Judgmental Attitude: Approach others without judgement, accepting them as they are. Avoid imposing your own beliefs or expectations on them. By cultivating a non-judgmental attitude, you create a space for open and authentic communication.

14. Vulnerability: Allow yourself to be vulnerable in your interactions. Share your thoughts, emotions, and experiences authentically, and encourage others to do the same. Sharing vulnerabilities fosters trust and strengthens relationships.

15. Empathy: Cultivate empathy by putting yourself in others' shoes and genuinely understanding their feelings and experiences. Show compassion and support, which encourages a reciprocal exchange of empathy and facilitates congruence.

16. Personal Growth: Rogers believed that personal growth is an ongoing process and a natural outcome of congruence. Here are some strategies for fostering personal growth:

17. Openness to Experience: Be open to new ideas, perspectives, and experiences. Embrace opportunities for learning and growth, as they expand your self-concept and lead to personal development.

18. Embracing Change: Recognize that change is a natural part of life. Embrace the challenges and uncertainties that come with change, as they offer valuable opportunities for personal growth and self-discovery.

19. Taking Responsibility: Take responsibility for your own choices, actions, and emotions. Acknowledge that you have the power to shape your own life and make positive changes. This sense of agency empowers personal growth.

20. Seeking Feedback: Seek feedback from trusted individuals who can provide constructive insights about your strengths and areas for improvement. Actively engage with feedback to facilitate personal growth and further align your self-concept with your experiences.

Erik Erikson, a prominent developmental psychologist, proposed a theory of psychosocial development that spans across the entire lifespan. He suggested that individuals go through eight distinct stages, each characterised by a unique psychosocial conflict or challenge. Here are Erikson's stages of psychosocial development:

1. Trust vs. Mistrust (Infancy, 0-1 year): In the first year of life, infants develop a sense of trust or mistrust depending on how well their needs for care, comfort, and nurturance are met. A nurturing and consistent caregiving environment fosters a sense of trust, while neglect or inconsistency may lead to mistrust.

2. Autonomy vs. Shame and Doubt (Early Childhood, 1-3 years): During this stage, children start asserting their independence and autonomy. Encouragement and support for their exploration and decision-making help them develop a sense of autonomy. If they face excessive criticism or control, they may develop shame and doubt about their abilities.

3. Initiative vs. Guilt (Preschool, 3-6 years): In the preschool years, children begin to take on more responsibility and assertiveness in their actions. They develop a sense of initiative by actively engaging in play and exploration. However, if their efforts are consistently met with disapproval or punishment, they may experience guilt and suppress their desires.

4. Industry vs. Inferiority (School Age, 6-11 years): School-age children strive to acquire new skills and engage in meaningful tasks. Success in these endeavours leads to a sense of industry and competence. However, if they experience consistent failure or receive excessive criticism, they may develop feelings of inferiority and inadequacy.

5. Identity vs. Role Confusion (Adolescence, 12-18 years): During adolescence, individuals explore and develop a sense of personal identity. They seek to understand who they are, their values, beliefs, and life goals. Successful resolution of this stage results in a clear and coherent sense of identity. Failure to establish an identity can lead to role confusion and a lack of direction.

6. Intimacy vs. Isolation (Early Adulthood, 18-40 years): In early adulthood, individuals form intimate relationships and develop deep connections with others. They seek to establish long-term, meaningful relationships based on trust, love, and commitment. Failure to establish intimacy may lead to feelings of isolation and loneliness.

7. Generativity vs. Stagnation (Middle Adulthood, 40-65 years): Middle-aged individuals focus on contributing to society and leaving a legacy. They engage in productive work, raise families, and participate in activities that benefit future generations. Those who

are unable to find meaning and purpose may experience a sense of stagnation.

8. Integrity vs. Despair (Late Adulthood, 65+ years): In the final stage of life, individuals reflect on their accomplishments and evaluate their life's meaning and purpose. Successfully resolving this stage leads to a sense of integrity and wisdom. However, individuals who harbour regrets or feel unfulfilled may experience feelings of despair.

9. It is important to note that Erikson's theory acknowledges that individuals may revisit and work on unresolved conflicts from previous stages throughout their lives. The successful resolution of each stage contributes to the development of a healthy and well-rounded individual.

One exercise inspired by Erik Erikson's theory of psychosocial development is the "identity exploration" process. This exercise encourages individuals to reflect on their values, interests, talents, and aspirations in order to consciously shape their identity.

Identity exploration is particularly relevant during Erikson's fifth stage of psychosocial development, known as identity versus role confusion. During adolescence and young adulthood, individuals go through a period of identity formation where they explore various roles and possibilities. This process continues throughout life as people encounter new experiences and challenges that shape their sense of self.

The exercise begins with individuals engaging in self-reflection and introspection. They are encouraged to explore their personal values, what is meaningful to them, and what they aspire to achieve. This involves examining their beliefs, principles, and priorities. Individuals can ask themselves questions such as:

1. What are my core values and beliefs?

2. What activities or interests bring me joy?

3. What are my talents and strengths?

4. What goals and aspirations do I have for my personal and professional life?

5. What roles do I see myself in (e.g., as a partner, parent, friend, professional)?

6. How do my values and aspirations align with the choices I have made so far?

Once individuals have reflected on these questions, they can engage in active exploration of different roles, beliefs, and experiences. This involves trying out new activities, taking on different responsibilities, and exposing themselves to diverse perspectives. By actively engaging in new experiences, individuals can gather information about themselves and the world around them, allowing them to shape their identity more consciously.

This process of identity exploration may involve:

1. Trying new activities: Individuals can explore new hobbies, join clubs or organisations, or take up new interests. By engaging in diverse experiences, individuals can learn more about themselves, their preferences, and their passions.

2. Seeking diverse perspectives: Individuals can actively seek out different perspectives by engaging in conversations with people from different backgrounds, cultures, and life experiences. This helps broaden their understanding of the world and challenge their own beliefs and assumptions.

3. Setting goals and pursuing aspirations: Individuals can set specific goals aligned with their values and interests and actively work towards achieving them. This process involves planning, taking action, and adapting as necessary. Through pursuing their aspirations,

individuals gain a deeper understanding of their capabilities and desires.

4. Embracing challenges and taking risks: Stepping outside of one's comfort zone and embracing challenges is an important aspect of identity exploration. By taking risks and facing new situations, individuals can discover hidden strengths and overcome obstacles, which contributes to their personal growth and self-understanding.

5. Reflecting and evaluating: Throughout the process of identity exploration, individuals should regularly reflect on their experiences, assess their growth, and evaluate how well their choices align with their evolving sense of self. This ongoing self-reflection allows for adjustments and refinements in their identity formation.

Monks

As we get ever further more introspective and quiet, we MUST look toward monks as an extreme example of this.

Monks seem to have nailed the mindfulness gambit, so how DO they do it?!

1. Mindfulness and Meditation: One of the key practices of monks is mindfulness meditation. This practice involves cultivating present-moment awareness and non-judgmental attention. Anyone can incorporate mindfulness into their daily life by setting aside a few minutes each day for meditation or practising mindfulness during routine activities like walking, eating, or washing dishes. This can help cultivate a sense of inner calm and focus.

2. Simplicity and Minimalism: Monks live with simplicity, often owning few material possessions and prioritising what is essential. You can adopt a minimalist mindset by decluttering your living space,

opting for quality over quantity in your belongings, and being mindful of your consumption habits. Simplifying your life can create more mental space, reduce stress, and allow you to focus on what truly matters.

3. Reflection and Self-Inquiry: Taking time for introspection and self-reflection is a valuable practice for personal growth. You can create a habit of journaling, engaging in deep contemplation, or seeking quiet moments for self-inquiry. Asking yourself meaningful questions about your values, goals, and purpose can help you gain clarity and develop a stronger sense of self.

4. Establishing Routines and Rituals: Monks follow structured routines that provide a sense of order and purpose. While you may not need to adhere to a monastic schedule, establishing daily or weekly routines and rituals can bring a sense of stability and meaning to your life. This could include setting aside dedicated time for self-care, physical exercise, reading, or engaging in creative pursuits.

5. Community and Connection: Although monks live in intentional communities, you can foster a sense of community and connection in your everyday life. Engage in activities that allow you to connect with like-minded individuals, participate in meaningful conversations, or contribute to your community through volunteering or supporting others. Building supportive relationships and finding a sense of belonging can enhance your overall wellbeing.

Are You a Monk?

In appreciation of monks

First up is a practical step and, like some of the points I've made, it leans towards the monk-ish.

Here's one journey of monkishness that has helped me.

When I was young, I concerned myself with what to wear.

As a teenager and then in my early twenties, I perused the men's section of Top Man and River Island, fingering through t-shirt sections, hoping to chance upon just the right image or slogan that would clearly signify to females in my age bracket that I was cool. That I was hip. That *I got it*. 'This cool t-shirt will surely secure boobs', I thought to myself.

I did this kind of thing for some time, before realising that I was being an idiot. This is not to say that people who care about fashion or what they wear are idiots: I was being an idiot because I was the one worried about the representation of self – for no reason.

From that point on, I decided to only wear the same thing – or at least the same type of thing. Plain clothes with no slogan, nor any image, stripe, pattern or diversity or any kind: a uniform. A coat, jumper or t-shirt in black, blue or green. Trousers in grey or dark blue. Comfortable shoes. Cheap versions, bought from supermarkets.

These have saved me huge amounts of money, as well as hours of clothes shopping and more hours of anguish. Again, if you like clothes shopping and dressing yourself up, then it's not a concern. But if you've ever thought 'oh no, I have nothing to wear' or been concerned at not being able to afford an item, then this can help.

This is especially true if you have ever wondered what exact combination of apparel would best demonstrate *who you are* and what you present to the world. Causing yourself concern in this way is odd: no one cares.

The kind of people that you want in your life won't care about what you wear – and the other type are far more concerned with how *they* are demonstrating *who they are* via the clothes they are wearing that day.

I understand that this was easier for me, as a man, because of the way society still regards expectations of how men and women can/should/do look. Even when I stepped out of the norms, it made people uncomfortable (as in they judged me). This includes not wearing a suit in an office and not wearing a fancy suit or tuxedo-type-of-thing as a wedding. Such simple, meaningless deviations from clothing expectation caused alarm. But it was alarm in others – that's their life experience that they're going to have to come to terms with. This is just one tiny example (or a *microcosm* if you're a thesaurus kind of writer) of how living life as the most you perturbs and disturbs others

All of us dressed in uniform, like monks, is a scene from a post-apocalyptic movie. I am not advocating the suppression of identity, style or fun. But dressing in uniform, like monks, is also a scene from a temple. Monks do seem to be in comfortable acceptance of who they are and their self identity.

They have also realised that their own form of 'self care' is to remove any modern nonsense from life. Now, this does not mean that they should be completely admired: any rule-based system will have its flaws, essentially being boiled down to a 'do this, don't do that' way of thinking.

Let's not get into the entire topic of religion, because this book isn't about that.

Yet, we can say that, despite most of the big religions having a general idea of goodness, there still seems something lacking in the real world practice. Specifically, if all of the people on Earth who said they were religious spent all of their time helping the needy, then there would be much less needy people around.

But it's not a realistic expectation, because they also want to live modern lives and have nice things.

Therein we are led to the question to have in your mind so that you may be able to become the most you: would you be happy to live like a monk?

Attachment Theory

Changing lanes! We change lanes here and look at another aspect in the emotional-mental mix: attachment theory.

Learning will help us. So what is Attachment Theory?

Attachment theory posits that the way individuals attach to others in adulthood is closely linked to their early attachment experiences as children.

Researchers have identified four distinct attachment styles: secure, avoidant, anxious, and disorganised.

Recognizing one's attachment style can serve as a crucial first step in strengthening relationships and fostering self-awareness.

1. Secure individuals exhibit low levels of avoidance and anxiety. They are comfortable with intimacy, have a positive view of themselves and their partners, and are not preoccupied with the relationship. They value both independence and interdependence, and they communicate their emotions and needs effectively. Secure individuals are empathetic, forgiving, and capable of managing conflicts constructively. As parents, they are sensitive, warm, and responsive, leading their children to develop secure attachments.

2. On the other hand, avoidant individuals exhibit high levels of avoidance but low levels of anxiety. They struggle with emotional closeness and opt for independence. They have difficulty depending on others or allowing others to depend on them. Avoidant individuals often communicate intellectually rather than emotionally and tend to avoid conflict until it escalates. They may appear emotionally distant, self-sufficient, and stoic. As parents, they may be emotionally unavailable and detached, leading to children with avoidant attachments.

3. Anxious individuals exhibit low levels of avoidance but high levels of anxiety. They crave closeness and intimacy but constantly worry about rejection and abandonment. They often seek reassurance and may exhibit clingy behaviours, which can push their partners away. Anxious individuals may ruminate about unresolved past issues, which affects their present relationships. They tend to be emotionally reactive, argumentative, and controlling, with poor personal boundaries. Communication may be characterised by blame and lack of collaboration. As parents, they may display inconsistent attunement and their children are more likely to develop anxious attachments.

4. Lastly, disorganised individuals have an unresolved mindset and experience fear triggered by memories of prior traumas. They struggle to tolerate emotional closeness and may exhibit abusive and dysfunctional relationship patterns. Disorganised individuals often have intrusive and frightening traumatic memories, which can lead to dissociation and severe mental health issues. They may engage in antisocial behaviour, lacking empathy and remorse. As parents, they are likely to mistreat their children and recreate unresolved attachment patterns. Children of disorganised individuals often develop disorganised attachments themselves.

What are the theories criticisms though?

1. Lack of Cultural Context: One criticism is that attachment theory primarily reflects the experiences and behaviours of individuals from Western, individualistic cultures. The theory may not adequately capture the diversity of attachment patterns and behaviours across different cultures and societies. Cultural factors such as collectivism, communal child-rearing practices, and different norms around

independence and interdependence may shape attachment patterns differently.

2. Simplistic Categorization: Critics argue that the classification of attachment styles into discrete categories oversimplifies the complexity of human attachment. Human relationships are multifaceted and dynamic, and individuals may exhibit a combination of attachment behaviours depending on the context and relationships. Viewing attachment as a fixed trait fails to capture the potential for change and adaptation over time.

3. Overemphasis on Early Experiences: Attachment theory places significant emphasis on early childhood experiences, particularly the relationship with the primary caregiver. Critics argue that this focus neglects the role of later experiences and social contexts in shaping attachment patterns. Factors such as peer relationships, cultural influences, and life events in adulthood can also impact attachment dynamics.

4. Lack of Gender Considerations: Attachment theory has been criticised for its limited consideration of gender differences in attachment patterns. Some argue that gender roles and societal expectations may influence attachment styles differently for men and women. For example, cultural norms of independence and self-reliance may lead to different expressions of attachment needs and behaviours between genders.

5. Nature vs. Nurture Debate: There is ongoing debate regarding the relative influence of genetics and environment in shaping attachment styles. While attachment theory primarily focuses on the impact of early caregiving experiences, critics argue that genetic factors and innate temperament may also play a role in the formation of attachment patterns. The nature vs. nurture debate highlights the complex interplay

between biological and environmental factors in attachment development.

6. Limited Predictive Power: Critics question the extent to which attachment styles in childhood accurately predict attachment patterns in adulthood. Some argue that attachment patterns can change over time, influenced by various life experiences, therapy, and personal growth. Therefore, the predictive power of attachment theory in determining long-term relationship outcomes and mental health is debated.

Movies and Love

We've looked at Attachment Theory because it is a thing that exists in the realm of romantic psychology. It's common sense that the relationships you see growing up affect how you view relationships when you are grown up.

There's also movies and TV. These are the things that shape entire brain belief systems about all life.

1. Unrealistic Portrayals: Movies like "The Notebook" (2004) often depict an idealised and passionate love story that can create unrealistic expectations for real-life relationships. The film showcases a perfect, all-consuming romance that may set unattainable standards for many viewers.

2. Narrow Representations: The lack of diversity in popular media can be seen in movies such as "The Proposal" (2009), which predominantly features heterosexual relationships. The underrepresentation of LGBTQ+ relationships in mainstream films can contribute to feelings of exclusion and invisibility for individuals who do not identify with the traditional narrative.

3. Relationship Violence and Toxicity: The "Twilight" series (2008-2012) has faced criticism for romanticising an unhealthy and possessive

relationship between the main characters. Edward's controlling and stalking behaviours are often seen as problematic, yet the series garnered a large following, potentially influencing perceptions of what constitutes a desirable relationship.

4. Unrealistic Expectations of Love: The movie "Crazy, Stupid, Love" (2011) portrays an idealised version of love and romance, where grand gestures and serendipitous moments abound. The whole film is shockingly sexist and it can contribute to the belief that love should always be thrilling and exciting, potentially overshadowing the importance of everyday commitment and communication in real relationships.

5. Comparisons and Self-Esteem: The film "13 Going on 30" (2004) explores the concept of comparing one's own life and relationships to an idealised vision of success. The protagonist's desire for a picture-perfect life can fuel unrealistic expectations and dissatisfaction with real-life experiences, leading to lowered self-esteem and happiness.

6. Influence on Gender Roles and Expectations: The classic film "Grease" (1978) perpetuates traditional gender roles and stereotypes, depicting women as submissive and dependent on men for validation. The portrayal of Danny's aggressive pursuit of Sandy can reinforce unequal power dynamics and contribute to unhealthy relationship dynamics.

You know what, here's 5 more:

1. Unrealistic Portrayals: "Pretty Woman" (1990) often comes up in discussions about unrealistic portrayals of relationships. The film presents a fairy tale-like narrative where a wealthy businessman falls in love with a sex worker and they live happily ever after. This romanticised depiction may create unrealistic expectations about love and relationships.

2. Relationship Violence and Toxicity: "Fifty Shades of Grey" (2015) has faced criticism for romanticising an abusive and controlling relationship between the main characters. The film's portrayal of BDSM dynamics without proper consent and communication has sparked concerns about the normalisation of unhealthy relationship behaviours.

3. Unrealistic Expectations of Love: In "Sleepless in Seattle" (1993), the characters fall in love without even meeting each other until the end. This romantic comedy perpetuates the notion of love at first sight and goes for grand gestures, potentially leading to unrealistic expectations of instant and effortless connections in real-life relationships.

4. Comparisons and Self-Esteem: "The Devil Wears Prada" (2006) features a storyline where the protagonist's personal relationships suffer due to her demanding career. This depiction may contribute to the belief that career success comes at the expense of personal happiness, leading to comparisons and potential dissatisfaction in real-life relationships.

5. Influence on Gender Roles and Expectations: The James Bond franchise, including films like "Goldfinger" (1964), has been criticised for perpetuating traditional gender roles and objectifying women. The portrayal of Bond as a suave, womanising spy and the objectification of female characters can reinforce unequal power dynamics and contribute to problematic expectations within relationships.

Last 4, but I mean really:

1. Relationship Violence and Toxicity: "Gone Girl" (2014) showcases a toxic and manipulative relationship. The film's depiction of emotional manipulation and violence can glamorise unhealthy behaviours and contribute to normalising toxic relationship dynamics.

2. Unrealistic Expectations of Love: "The Princess Bride" (1987) is a beloved fairy tale that presents a fantastical and idealised version of love. The film's emphasis on true love conquering all can create unrealistic expectations and downplay the challenges and complexities of real relationships.

3. Comparisons and Self-Esteem: "Mean Girls" (2004) explores the high school social hierarchy and the impact of comparison and validation. The film's focus on popularity and appearance can perpetuate a culture of comparison and negatively affect self-esteem, particularly in the context of romantic relationships.

4. Influence on Gender Roles and Expectations: "Dirty Dancing" (1987) portrays traditional gender roles where the male lead takes charge and the female lead follows. While the film has iconic dance sequences, it can reinforce gender stereotypes and contribute to rigid expectations within relationships.

So as you can see, you didn't really have much chance from the ages of toddler to teen, that most of what you saw was unrealistic and just nonsense. And to be fair, terrible movie making as well. Except Dirty Dancing. Innate charm outweighs non-believability in this case.

So, in terms of both controlling and conflicted, not much else is as strong as love.

'Look at this awesome and amazing thing, other people have it, and when they get it it's the BEST THING EVER. EVER! The End.'

This is alongside 'it' being an inexplicable, unexplainable thing. Most things you are told you desire are at least ACTUAL THINGS, not concepts that no person on Earth can universally define.

How can you be in control of your heart in a conflicted and controlling world?

Method One: Time

Does time really exist? Does love?

Yes. Next damn fool question.

But really though, we are told that love is a thing that will basically, pretty much occur if two people meet each other and then quite like each other and then actually really want to hump each other and then live together. Then boom: love.

The other problem is that this happens in the age bracket known as the twenties.

The problem with being in your 20s in some societies: you've been socially groomed into thinking that once you get to around 22, you're an adult. You have finished education, you move out (or should at least desperately want to move out) from home and are ready to start a relationship that may very well lead to marriage and creating new humans and staying together forever because you like each other lots. Oh also your entire life of employment might have been defined already for you, so keep going and get more promotions and money later.

It's essentially saying; 'although you're completely new to the adult world, make all of the seminal life-decisions right away!'.

It's not that anyone in their 20s simply 'knows less' or is immature – this is not someone who is older saying that 'the young are bad'. It's about not feeling obligated to be an adult, not feeling the need to commit to anything and most of all it's about pressure and how you deal with it.

One of the most ridiculous things that people do in their teens is say they are in love. A teenager who says they're in love would refute this. They really know love. They know other teens don't – but they do. Someone in their 20s who hears a teen say they are in love would think it's silly – while being sure that, because they broke the age 20 threshold, their love declarations are now entirely accurate. This is how divorce happens. Well, one reason (the other reason is that marriage is an unnatural concept, but this isn't about that).

In some so-called "developing" societies around the world, people are heavily pressured into marriage – and they hate it. It causes enormous damage to mental health, both in the process and as a consequence in life. If you're not living in such a society then you may not need to essentially force yourself into marriage because you really like each other at that moment in time.

At any age, it takes a long time to get to know someone and trust someone.

I can't think of a famous movie in which two people take around 10 to 15 years to slowly get to know each other before making any 'promise' to do all the love things like complete monogamy and respect and taking care of the person when they are sick, or being a dick.

It may be better for you to make this the movie of your life - wherever possible. Not the being a dick part, but the realising that it takes over a decade to truly know someone, let alone yourself.

Method Two: Reduce Emotion

Real, notable, noticeable, heady, hormonal, survivalistic, valuable emotions like love.

Heroic.

The pop star emoting on stage, the sports person reaching a pinnacle, the movie hero fighting to battle back against all odds.

These are the most glamorous notions of being human. But, ask yourself this: when have emotions *specifically helped* you do something in life?

If something actually needs to get DONE, then it's often removing emotions that is effective and efficient.

Modern nonsense sees us being told to combine passion with our paying job. We are told to 'own' projects - but also to be a complete team player and don't take things personally. In reality, we can be our most professional selves by reducing emotion, particularly in conflict.

Work can be such a strange environment. It's a group of people whom you are often thrown in with randomly. You are 'supposed to' get quite close, be open and share who you are. But you are also expected to continually show your best side. Turn up at the office well-groomed, be nice, not have any failings or cynicisms and laugh at every joke made by someone who is in a more senior position. If you're unfortunate, then some of those around you can be difficult. Those more senior in the hierarchy can be egotistical. There can be passive-aggressive (or just aggressive) comments, emails, and the tactical weekend message. From a boss, this might start with 'don't reply now, but…'.

Between colleagues, it never pays to engage in email nastiness. No one has ever made a considered response to an email argument/accusation that results in the other person saying 'oh yeah, you're right, sorry'. It only leads to more baiting and silliness.

Work is distinct from other situations, where it can be possibly easier to do nothing – otherwise known as taking the high road. Taking the high road, in my experience, is always the best thing to do. Old expressions are truisms – often centuries old – because they work. Take the high road and 'don't go down to their level' are two phrases that provide excellent imagery of what you need to do and why.

But at work, it's about your income, your livelihood. We've talked about removing ego and setting out your stall. Sometimes, grinning and bearing it is a reality that adults need to experience. A hypothetical action in your head is a good test of what the responses might be. If you said the words, what might be the consequence? Any response to your action might be worse than if you'd have done nothing at all.

In the world of parenting, unconditional love is a social assumption. But even if you want to be a good parent, then 'love' isn't the certain way to parent best - hence the phrase 'tough love': part of parenting is showing the child the real world, and that it won't always love them.

In other areas of life, view emotion first, rather than bathe in it.

Split your mind into different parts - two should be enough in this case. Don't simply 'feel' and then bask in said feeling. Recognise a feeling but then look at it from all angles as your second self.

Don't assume the emotions will actually help you be the most you. They might be helping someone else be the most them.

Method Three: Look at 'Trust' Weirdly

Trust is a kind of emotion but also an abstract action. Or it could be a literal action, for example if you trust someone to hold your baby but then you realise they are in fact a lion. Oops!

Again; we are told it's good. Loyalty, honour, trust. King Arthur. Lions. Sword in the Stone. Disney. Trust.

Trust falls.

"You've got to trust people."

"I've invested in a trust."

"Do you trust your partner?"

Well, this is all silly but a good phrase is: trust arrives on foot but leaves on horseback.

The internet reveals countless sources that either say or hedge their bets on trusting people being good, and if you don't trust people, that's bad.

If we remove emotion and think about how to be our most selves then what about this question: what is really and truly good for you by trusting ANYONE.

Now it may be said that if you just did not trust anyone then you would be anxious, paranoid, worried and just bad.

But that suggests a rather extreme state whereby you are assumed you be a snivelling wreck and/or other people are specifically going to do you harm.

This is different from trust.

Not trusting anyone could simply be a calm and methodical way of essentially never being surprised or shocked.

Or never putting yourself in a particular situation - just because society says you should (even though they are not the ones with something to lose by YOU trusting others) - whereby you would lose heavily all due to the arbitrary concept of trust.

Now this is not advocating a life whereby you definitely absolutely do not trust anyone.

It's keeping the concept in mind and, most importantly, realising that if you go for trust, then it be on your terms. This can mean YOU decide how long or how many occasions it takes for you to trust another person. It could be 10 years or 20 years. Why not? Or, just trust everyone easily. This book isn't about this book, it's about you. Your life, your rules.

Method Four: Love Old Sayings

So there was the trust one above. There's also:

Only fools rush in.

Absence makes the heart grow fonder.

A hedge between keeps friendship green.

If you are in a relationship, then for the love of God, have time apart. (that's actually my quote)

On balance, monogamy probably does make life and the world a more organised, less chaotic place. The world that we've created now lends itself to the state of monogamy, with individual family units.

However in a utopia where everyone and everything is close to perfect, polygamy would be more 'natural', relevant to our throbbing biological urges and, in a nice way, our ability to procreate and love.

So, back to the reality of monogamy - whether you like it or not. With working from home and with technology, couples are in each other's faces.

Anyone is annoying when you see them all the time.

Simple time apart is healthy.

Not just romantic partners (if there is romance left after seeing each other too much), but a parent will find their own baby or child annoying. Even 5 minutes out of the house from the crying baby changes an entire mental state.

Friendships too. The closer people get, the less boundaries they have and so their innate yuckiness of humanity will emerge. People who seem really good 'mates' and are nice to each other often see each other occasionally and in set environments.

Love is pushed upon us by society as something that is eternally good; but we can't have Christmas every day. To be honest even once a year is getting a bit much.

Keep it rare, keep it traditional. Or love everyone all the time. Over to you.

PART THREE
YOUR GUT

Your Gut

Do you have the guts? What's your gut feel? These are old phrases of no definitive origin, thus showing that there was a gut feel about our gut feel hundreds of years ago.

Intuition, nous, perhaps with a little gumption and a sprinkling of pluck.

The interesting thing is that science has helped us. Thanks, science! The boffins over at Generic Science Lab discovered that there is a 'gut-brain axis'.

Honestly, I typed 'but-brain' as a typo TWICE, which looks like butt-brain and must refer back to our old pal Freud.

Anyway:

The gut-brain axis refers to the bidirectional communication system between the gastrointestinal tract (the gut) and the brain.

This communication occurs through various pathways, including the nervous system, immune system, and the release of chemical messengers.

The gut-brain axis plays a crucial role in influencing not only digestive processes but also cognitive and emotional functions. Here's a detailed explanation of the gut-brain axis:

1. Nervous System Communication: The gut and the brain are connected through a network of nerves, including the vagus nerve, which is the primary communication pathway between the two. The vagus nerve carries signals bidirectionally, allowing the brain to influence gut function and vice versa. This connection enables the transmission of sensory information, such as pain or discomfort in the gut, to the brain, as well as the regulation of gut motility, secretion, and blood flow.

2. Neurotransmitters and Hormones: The gut and the brain communicate through the release of chemical

messengers, including neurotransmitters and hormones. For example, serotonin, a neurotransmitter associated with mood regulation, is primarily produced in the gut. It influences not only gastrointestinal function but also plays a role in modulating mood, appetite, and sleep. Other neurotransmitters, such as gamma-aminobutyric acid (GABA) and dopamine, are also involved in gut-brain communication.

3. Microbiota-Gut-Brain Axis: The gut microbiota, the community of microorganisms residing in the gastrointestinal tract, also plays a crucial role in the gut-brain axis. The gut microbiota can produce neurotransmitters, such as serotonin, and release metabolites that can directly or indirectly affect brain function. Moreover, the gut microbiota interacts with the immune system and produces molecules that can influence brain health and function.

4. Immune System Interactions: The gut has a significant influence on the immune system, and immune cells in the gut can communicate with immune cells in the brain. Inflammation in the gut can trigger immune responses and produce pro-inflammatory cytokines that can impact brain function. This immune system communication between the gut and the brain is thought to play a role in various psychiatric and neurological disorders.

5. The relationship between the gut and thoughts, including the concept of "gut feel," has historical references that date back to ancient civilizations. The phrase "gut feel" or "gut instinct" refers to the intuitive sense or feeling that arises from the gut and influences decision-making. While the exact mechanisms behind this phenomenon are not fully understood, emerging research suggests that the gut's ability to communicate with the brain may contribute to these intuitive sensations.

Scientifically, the gut communicates with the brain through the pathways described above.

The gut's sensory information, such as signals related to gut discomfort or hunger, is transmitted to the brain, which can influence thoughts, emotions, and decision-making processes.

The release of neurotransmitters and hormones from the gut, along with the influence of the gut microbiota and immune system, can modulate brain function and potentially impact cognitive processes and mood.

Intuition?

Intuition was remarked upon by that Plato fellow you've been hearing so much about.

Plato and Aristotle, prominent ancient Greek philosophers, had distinct theories regarding the concept of "nous," which can be understood as intellect or intuition.

Plato, in his dialogues, discussed the concept of nous as a higher form of knowledge that transcends the physical senses.

According to Plato, nous is a faculty of the soul that allows individuals to perceive universal truths and forms, which exist beyond the material world. He viewed nous as a form of intuitive understanding that goes beyond ordinary sensory perception and rational thought. For Plato, the ultimate goal was to attain knowledge through the contemplation of eternal truths accessible through nous.

Aristotle, a student of Plato, had a different perspective on nous. He considered it as a rational faculty of the mind that is based on experience and perception. Aristotle viewed nous as a higher form of intellect that enables individuals to grasp first principles and make deductive inferences.

He believed that nous is an innate capacity of the human mind and plays a crucial role in the process of acquiring knowledge.

Aristotle's understanding of nous was more grounded in empirical observations and logical reasoning.

While Plato and Aristotle differed in their views on the nature of nous, both philosophers recognized the importance of reason and intuition in understanding the world.

They acknowledged that human cognition involves more than sensory perception and logical analysis. Intuition, as embodied in the concept of nous, allows individuals to access deeper insights and truths that go beyond what can be directly observed or logically deduced.

Back to more modern science, Cognitive Psychologists have studied intuitive processes and identified two general types of intuition: implicit and explicit intuition. Implicit intuition refers to the rapid, automatic, and unconscious processing of information, often based on prior experiences and expertise.

It allows individuals to make quick judgments and decisions without deliberate thought. Explicit intuition, on the other hand, involves conscious and deliberate processing of information, drawing on patterns, heuristics, and contextual cues.

Neuroscience research has revealed that intuitive processing involves the interaction of various brain regions, including the prefrontal cortex, amygdala, and insula. These regions play a role in pattern recognition, emotional processing, and integrating sensory information, contributing to intuitive judgments and decision-making.

Furthermore, studies have shown that intuition can be honed and developed through expertise and deliberate practice in specific domains.

Experts in various fields, such as medicine, chess, and music, often rely on their intuitive abilities to make accurate and rapid judgments based on their extensive knowledge and experience.

And back to Plato. For Plato, the ultimate goal of philosophical inquiry and intellectual pursuit was to attain knowledge through the contemplation of eternal truths, which he believed were accessible through the faculty of nous.

Plato saw the physical world as a realm of imperfection and transience, where objects and phenomena are subject to change and decay. However, he posited that beyond the physical realm lies a higher reality, the world of Forms or Ideas. These Forms are perfect, eternal, and unchanging essences that represent the true nature of things. According to Plato, genuine knowledge and understanding come from grasping these universal Forms, which exist independently of individual instances in the physical world.

Plato argued that nous, or intellect, is the highest faculty of the human soul and the means by which individuals can apprehend these eternal truths. Through the contemplation of the Forms, individuals can attain knowledge that goes beyond sensory perception and the realm of opinion. This knowledge is considered more reliable and superior to the knowledge obtained through empirical observations or logical reasoning.

According to Plato, the process of attaining knowledge through nous involves a dialectical method of inquiry.

Through dialogue and questioning, individuals are encouraged to critically examine their beliefs and opinions and to engage in a philosophical search for truth. This process aims to move beyond mere appearances and opinions toward a deeper understanding of the underlying Forms that give rise to the physical manifestations.

1. Plato believed that the philosopher, as someone who has developed their intellectual faculties and purified their soul, is best suited to engage in this contemplative pursuit of eternal truths.

2. The philosopher, through their disciplined study and reflection, can elevate their nous to a higher level of

understanding and achieve a direct apprehension of the Forms.

3. Plato's view of knowledge and the role of nous in its attainment has profound implications for his philosophy as a whole.

4. He argued that the world of Forms provides the foundation for moral values, justice, beauty, and the ideal organisation of society. By aligning oneself with the eternal truths accessible through nous, individuals can attain wisdom and live a virtuous life.

5. It is important to note that Plato's concept of nous and his emphasis on the contemplation of eternal truths have been the subject of scholarly debate and interpretation.

6. The exact nature of the Forms and the process of contemplation can vary among different interpretations of Plato's philosophy.

Nonetheless, Plato's notion of attaining knowledge through the contemplation of eternal truths accessible through nous represents a central theme in his philosophy. It highlights his belief in the existence of a transcendent realm of truth and the transformative power of intellectual inquiry in guiding individuals toward wisdom and understanding.

Plato believed that the eternal truths, also known as the Forms or Ideas, are the ultimate reality and the source of genuine knowledge. These Forms are perfect and unchanging essences that exist independently of individual instances in the physical world.

According to Plato, the physical world that we perceive through our senses is a realm of imperfection and change.

1. Objects and phenomena in the physical world are mere reflections or imitations of the true Forms. For example, a beautiful flower in the physical world is an

imperfect copy of the Form of Beauty, which represents the true essence of beauty itself.

2. Plato identified various Forms representing different concepts, such as Beauty, Justice, Goodness, Truth, and Virtue.

3. The knowledge of these eternal truths, according to Plato, is not acquired through sensory perception or logical reasoning alone.

4. Instead, he believed that nous, the highest faculty of the human soul, is capable of directly apprehending these Forms through contemplation and philosophical inquiry.

5. Through the use of reason and dialectical methods, individuals can elevate their understanding and grasp the universal truths that underlie the changing world of appearances.

6. By aligning oneself with these eternal truths, individuals can strive for moral excellence, pursue justice, and live a virtuous life.

It is worth noting that Plato's exact conception of the Forms and their nature has been a subject of debate among scholars and philosophers. Some interpret the Forms as abstract entities that exist independently, while others see them as mental concepts or patterns that exist within the human mind.

Regardless of the specific interpretation, Plato's emphasis on the existence of eternal truths and their role in guiding human understanding remains a significant aspect of his philosophy.

And back to modern life.

Applying Plato's thinking directly to daily life in a modern world can be a meaningful endeavour, as it offers valuable insights into personal growth, ethical conduct, and the pursuit of success.

Here are some ways individuals can incorporate Plato's ideas into their lives and potentially achieve success:

1. Cultivate self-awareness: Plato chose the importance of self-examination and understanding one's own strengths, weaknesses, and inherent nature. By engaging in introspection and self-reflection, individuals can gain a deeper understanding of their abilities, passions, and purpose. This self-awareness can guide them in making choices aligned with their true selves, leading to a more fulfilling and successful life.

2. Pursue lifelong learning: Plato advocated for the pursuit of knowledge and the continuous quest for wisdom. In a modern context, this translates to valuing education, seeking new experiences, and engaging in intellectual and personal growth. By embracing a mindset of lifelong learning, individuals can expand their horizons, develop critical thinking skills, and adapt to the ever-changing demands of the world.

3. Strive for moral integrity: Plato believed that true success is not solely measured by external achievements but also by one's moral character. Integrating ethical principles into daily life is crucial. This involves acting with honesty, fairness, and compassion towards others. By practising integrity, individuals can build trust, foster healthy relationships, and contribute positively to their communities, thereby enhancing their chances of personal and professional success.

4. Embrace justice and fairness: Plato's concept of justice encourages individuals to act in accordance with the greater good and to treat others fairly. In a modern context, this means promoting equality, social justice, and respect for the rights and dignity of all individuals. By advocating for fairness and justice in their personal

and professional interactions, individuals can create a more inclusive and harmonious environment that supports personal growth and success for themselves and others.

5. Strive for balance and harmony: Plato emphasised the importance of inner harmony and balance among different aspects of the self. Applying this principle involves nurturing one's physical, mental, and emotional wellbeing. Balancing work, relationships, personal interests, and self-care allows individuals to maintain a sense of equilibrium, leading to increased productivity, fulfilment, and long-term success.

6. Embrace the pursuit of truth: Plato believed in the existence of eternal truths and the importance of seeking knowledge and understanding. In a modern world filled with information overload and conflicting opinions, individuals can apply Plato's thinking by cultivating critical thinking skills, questioning assumptions, and seeking reliable sources of information. By striving for truth and intellectual honesty, individuals can make informed decisions, avoid pitfalls of misinformation, and navigate complexities more effectively.

What does it mean to embrace truth?

This is where we come to the area that I find fascinating, because the very nature of the theory is in conflict with itself, and so we have discovered the lovely crack (so to speak), the fissure, the gap, the void, the faultline, the area of potential further discovery.

The guided research or findings at this point, if we were to research 'how does one pursue the truth', is to do things like increase our critical thinking and to practise intellectual humility.

These two things are great things that everyone should always do. If everyone did always do these two things, the world would be a better place, as fewer people would be so arrogant and self-serving. It is also very helpful in making us smarter, better at making decisions and more successful, the most us etc. etc.

HOWEVER, the standard guided examples of what else to do therefore becomes irrelevant and in turn become things that we either should question (at the very least) or specifically NOT do.

These things that we are told to do in order to pursue the truth are things like:

1. Stay open minded

2. Seek diverse opinions

3. Reflect on personal biases (different to intellectual humility)

4. Engage in continuous learning

Without context, and to be honest even with context, these things are in no way definitely positive things. And here is why, friend:

Being open minded is championed in the silly areas of modern-day society, namely the workplace. "Let's go into this with an open mind" is a good way of not saying "my idea might be shit so don't question it or I'll say you are not being open minded" or "this is basically pointless busywork and/or corporate nonsense but can we all please pretend that it's not?".

What if someone said "we're all going to do a workplace course on having good table manners. Let's go into this with open minds please!", then SURELY, you would think to yourself "this is cretinously retarded because I already know that and this is thusly a waste of my time." That's YOU in this example that thought of the phrase 'cretinously retarded', not I. I'd never say such a general phrase that everyone says, because it's bad to say that in any context.

And so we are led to the conclusion that we do not always need to be open-minded and that being open-minded can be a waste of time.

Diversity is funny because – much like some of the previously mentioned thinkers (Maslow, Freud et al) framed things in a context of positivity. I mean who wouldn't like positive diversity? What if someone offered you a GREATER range of sauces AND condiments with your meal? What if you could go on holiday to THREE places instead of ONE? IF diversity means more choice and variety and not being limited, then that's nice. If, however, diversity means 'different things are always inherently good', then by simple logic and common sense, I must disagree.

In England, for example, we are attempting to achieve gender equality. I don't have time for another 50,000 words on how this is going, but normal people agree that this must happen and that it is an eternal form of justice.

In other countries, they don't think this and they stop women from doing lots of things. You could even say that people in other places in the world have 'diverse' opinions on the role of women in society. Ditto lots of other things = mere diversity isn't good if the original thing was already really good.

This relates to personal biases. If you really wanted to just be silly, you might say that 'WESTERN' biases are really bad. You might argue, for God only knows what reason (figuratively), that 'my biases are bad, because biases are bad'. Bias: inclination OR prejudice for or against something. This can be silly because let's say that it could be called a 'bias' to believe that we must achieve full gender equality, not in terms of things like 'men and women are the same' but in terms of both men and women must have the same opportunities and be 'treated' equally with equal rights. This is in a sensible context, such as men and women should be paid the same for doing the same jobs, not that men should also get the same maternity leave as women, because it's women's bodies what does the baby-making aspect.

But this isn't about that at all, that was just a personal indulgence and also an example too.

The real point here is that you may have good, correct personal biases and you do not always need to challenge them, otherwise we risk ruining the advancements in society that generally relate to equality.

This relates to 'engaging in continuous learning' and the hyped emphasis that learning has in some areas of society. This might feel inconsistent to be said in a book that's about development and learning things, but I feel that we have to be careful with learning.

If we're not careful, then learning can be like the gym membership body aspect. We see others showing their bodies on social media so we pay for gym gear and gym memberships and then feel bad if we don't look like what they do.

Investing money and time in simple 'learning' is often done so that the person can tell others that they are learning. The risk is that you feel like everyone else is learning but you are not, or, you try but then give up because learning is boring. What really is there to learn in a real way? I think that enough people know the thing so that you don't always need to trouble yourself with learning it.

This is just why this is all framed as 'being the most you', not the best. Maybe the best you could indeed play the guitar and then everyone you've ever known would stand in the audience watching you be really soulful on stage with your guitar and then they would all love and respect you, but do you realise how many guitar lessons that would take to get there?

Being the most you is never about self-worship or arrogance but if the most you is already really nice then embracing truth can mean enhancing and emphasising your existing goodness

Collective Nous

How can it not be fascinating when different people in different places come up with the same ideas at the same time?

Of course, there can be a natural evolution of ideas, and things like inventions become possible when other science becomes known.

But there are enough cases of this to indicate that there is something of a collective nous.

There are several examples throughout history of individuals in different parts of the world independently developing similar ideas, inventions, or theories without direct communication.

These instances have often been attributed to the convergence of circumstances, shared cultural or environmental factors, or the universal nature of certain phenomena. Here are a few notable examples:

1. Independent Invention of Writing Systems: Sumerian Cuneiform (Mesopotamia) and Egyptian Hieroglyphs: Both writing systems emerged independently around 3200 BCE.

2. Mayan Glyphs (Mesoamerica): The Mayans developed their own writing system around 300 BCE.

3. Independent Discovery of Calculus: Isaac Newton (England) and Gottfried Wilhelm Leibniz (Germany): Newton and Leibniz independently developed calculus in the late 17th century, with both making significant contributions to the field.

4. Multiple Independent Inventions of the Telephone: Alexander Graham Bell (Scotland/Canada/USA) and Elisha Gray (USA): Bell and Gray filed patent applications for the telephone on the same day in 1876, unaware of each other's work.

87

5. Simultaneous Development of Evolutionary Theory: Charles Darwin (England) and Alfred Russel Wallace (England): Darwin and Wallace independently proposed the theory of evolution through natural selection in the mid-19th century.

6. Independent Discovery of the Law of Conservation of Energy: James Prescott Joule (England) and Julius von Mayer (Germany): Joule and Mayer independently formulated the concept of the conservation of energy in the mid-19th century.

It is worth noting that in many cases, while the ideas or inventions may appear similar or related, there are often subtle differences or variations in their approaches or implementations.

Additionally, these examples represent a fraction of instances where simultaneous or independent discovery has occurred, and there may be other lesser-known cases as well.

The phenomenon of independent discovery underscores the universality of human creativity, the shared nature of certain scientific or cultural developments, and the capacity of individuals to arrive at similar conclusions through observation, experimentation, and reasoning.

Here are some more:

1. Theory of General Relativity: Albert Einstein (Germany/Switzerland) and David Hilbert (Germany): Both Einstein and Hilbert independently developed the theory of general relativity in the early 20th century.

2. Decimal Number System: Ancient Egyptians, Babylonians, and Mayans: These civilizations independently developed their own systems of counting and numerical notation, including the concept of place value.

3. Zero in Mathematics: Ancient Indians and Mayans: The concept of zero was independently discovered and utilised by both ancient Indian mathematicians and Mayan mathematicians.

4. Paper Invention: Ancient Egyptians and Chinese: The Egyptians and Chinese independently invented paper, albeit using different materials and techniques.

5. Discovery of Neptune: John Couch Adams (England) and Urbain Le Verrier (France): Both Adams and Le Verrier independently predicted the existence and location of the planet Neptune based on mathematical calculations.

6. Theory of Plate Tectonics: Alfred Wegener (Germany) and Frank Bursley Taylor (United States): Wegener and Taylor independently proposed the theory of continental drift and plate tectonics.

7. Development of Photography: Louis Daguerre (France) and William Henry Fox Talbot (England): Daguerre and Talbot independently invented photographic processes in the 1830s.

8. Discovery of Insulin: Frederick Banting and Charles Best (Canada) and Nicolae Paulescu (Romania): Banting and Best, along with Paulescu, independently discovered insulin as a treatment for diabetes in the early 1920s.

The phenomenon of simultaneous or independent discoveries and inventions has intrigued researchers and scholars for many years.

Several theories have been proposed to explain this phenomenon, although it is important to note that these theories do not typically involve telepathy, as telepathy lacks scientific evidence and is considered outside the realm of mainstream scientific inquiry.

Here are a few theories that have been put forward:

89

1. Convergent Evolution of Ideas: This theory suggests that similar environmental, social, or technological conditions can lead to the development of similar ideas or solutions independently. It proposes that certain problems or challenges are universal, and different individuals or cultures may arrive at similar solutions due to shared circumstances or constraints.

2. Multiple Discovery Theory: According to this theory, the development of new ideas or inventions is a natural and inevitable consequence of human progress. It suggests that when the necessary knowledge, technology, or cultural context reaches a certain level, multiple individuals or groups are likely to make the same discovery or invention almost simultaneously.

3. Cultural Diffusion: This theory argues that ideas, knowledge, and inventions can spread across cultures through trade, migration, or cultural exchange. It suggests that the dissemination of information and cross-cultural interactions can lead to parallel developments in different regions.

4. Collective Unconscious: Proposed by Carl Jung, the concept of the collective unconscious suggests that there are shared archetypal patterns, symbols, and ideas that exist in the collective psyche of humanity. According to this theory, individuals can tap into this collective unconscious and access universal knowledge or insights, which may contribute to the occurrence of simultaneous discoveries.

The concept of the collective unconscious, proposed by Carl Jung, suggests that there are universal patterns, symbols, and ideas that are inherited and shared among all humans.

While the existence of the collective unconscious is a theoretical construct, it has influenced various fields, including psychology, spirituality, and creativity.

Here are some ideas on what individuals can learn from the concept of the collective unconscious:

1. Archetypal Patterns: The collective unconscious is said to contain archetypes, which are fundamental patterns of thoughts, behaviours, and emotions that are common to all humans. By understanding these archetypes, individuals can gain insights into their own motivations, desires, and fears. This self-awareness can aid personal growth and development.

2. Symbolic Language: The collective unconscious communicates through symbols and imagery. Exploring symbolism and interpreting dreams, myths, and art can provide individuals with a deeper understanding of themselves and the collective human experience. It can help them connect with universal themes and tap into the deeper layers of their psyche.

3. Transcending the Ego: The concept of the collective unconscious suggests that there is more to the human psyche than just individual consciousness. By recognizing the existence of this collective realm, individuals can transcend their ego-centric perspective and develop a sense of connectedness to something greater than themselves. This can foster empathy, compassion, and a broader perspective on life.

While the collective unconscious contains numerous archetypes, here are some of the most well-known and commonly discussed:

1. The Self: The archetype of the Self represents the wholeness and integration of the psyche. It symbolises the striving for completeness, individuation, and the realisation of one's true potential.

2. The Shadow: The Shadow archetype embodies the dark and repressed aspects of the psyche that are often considered unacceptable or undesirable. It represents

the unconscious elements, including instincts, impulses, and unresolved conflicts.

3. The Anima (in men) and Animus (in women): These archetypes represent the feminine aspects in men (anima) and the masculine aspects in women (animus). They symbolise the opposite gender qualities that exist within individuals and play a role in influencing relationships and inner balance.

4. The Persona: The Persona archetype refers to the social mask or facade that individuals present to the world. It represents the public image and the roles we adopt in different social contexts.

5. The Wise Old Man/Woman: This archetype represents wisdom, insight, and spiritual knowledge. It symbolises the quest for meaning, guidance, and the integration of wisdom gained through life experiences.

6. The Hero: The Hero archetype embodies the courageous and transformative aspects of human nature. It represents the journey of overcoming challenges, facing fears, and striving for personal growth and collective wellbeing.

7. The Trickster: The Trickster archetype represents the mischievous, unpredictable, and transformative aspects of human behaviour. It embodies the capacity for creative chaos, challenging societal norms, and breaking conventions.

8. The Mother: The Mother archetype symbolises nurturing, caring, and unconditional love. It represents the primal source of nourishment, protection, and emotional support.

9. The Father: The Father archetype embodies authority, guidance, and the protective aspect. It represents the principles of discipline, responsibility, and providing guidance and structure.

10. The Child: The Child archetype represents innocence, spontaneity, and potential for growth and creativity. It embodies the capacity for wonder, playfulness, and embracing new experiences.

It is important to note that these archetypes are not fixed or rigid categories but rather dynamic and evolving expressions of the collective unconscious.

They can manifest in various ways and have personal and cultural variations.

Additionally, individuals may resonate with different archetypes at different stages of their lives or in specific contexts.

As for tapping into the collective unconscious and influencing it with one's thoughts and actions, it is important to note that this is a topic of speculation and remains outside the realm of scientific validation. However, some practices that individuals may explore include:

1. Self-Reflection and Inner Work: Engaging in practices such as meditation, journaling, or contemplation can help individuals develop a deeper connection with their own subconscious and potentially access collective symbols and insights.

2. Creative Expression: Engaging in creative activities, such as art, music, or writing, can serve as a channel for tapping into the collective unconscious. Through creative expression, individuals can access deeper layers of their psyche and potentially connect with universal themes and archetypes.

3. Openness and Receptivity: Cultivating an open and receptive mindset can create a conducive environment for insights and inspiration to arise. Being open to different perspectives, exploring diverse cultural and artistic expressions, and embracing the unknown can

expand one's awareness and potentially tap into the collective unconscious.

Here are some real life lessons that are said to be derived from these archetypes:

1. Self-awareness and Integration: Understanding the archetype of the Self emphasises the importance of self-awareness and the pursuit of wholeness. By recognizing and integrating all aspects of oneself, individuals can foster a sense of balance and authenticity, leading to personal growth and wellbeing.

2. Embracing Shadow Work: Acknowledging and exploring the Shadow archetype can be transformative. By facing and accepting one's shadow aspects, individuals can cultivate self-compassion, resolve inner conflicts, and unlock their hidden potentials.

3. Embracing Balance and Harmony: Recognizing and integrating the anima and animus archetypes highlight the significance of embracing both feminine and masculine qualities within oneself, regardless of gender. Striving for balance and harmony between these aspects can promote healthier relationships and personal wholeness.

4. Authenticity and Persona: Understanding the Persona archetype encourages individuals to reflect on their public image and the roles they play in different contexts. By aligning the Persona with one's authentic self, individuals can cultivate genuine connections and live in alignment with their values.

5. Embracing Wisdom and Growth: The Wise Old Man/Woman archetype reminds individuals of the importance of lifelong learning, self-reflection, and embracing the wisdom gained from experiences. It encourages a mindset of continual growth, personal development, and spiritual exploration.

6. Courage and Transformation: The Hero archetype teaches individuals the value of facing challenges and embracing personal transformation. By summoning courage, individuals can overcome obstacles, pursue their dreams, and make a positive impact on themselves and others.

7. Embracing Creativity and Flexibility: The Trickster archetype highlights the importance of embracing creativity, spontaneity, and a flexible mindset. It encourages individuals to challenge conventions, think outside the box, and approach life with a sense of playfulness and curiosity.

8. Nurturing and Self-care: The Mother archetype is about the significance of nurturing oneself and others, practising self-care, and cultivating emotional wellbeing. It reminds individuals to foster a sense of compassion, kindness, and nourishment in their lives.

9. Responsibility and Guidance: The Father archetype underscores the importance of taking responsibility for one's actions, providing guidance, and establishing healthy boundaries. It encourages individuals to cultivate discipline, leadership qualities, and a sense of purpose.

10. Embracing Wonder and Growth: The Child archetype invites individuals to embrace a sense of wonder, playfulness, and curiosity in life. It encourages individuals to maintain a youthful spirit, embrace new experiences, and nurture their creativity.

By integrating these archetypal lessons into their lives, individuals can gain insights into their own psyche, cultivate self-awareness, and navigate their journey towards a healthier and more successful life.

It is important to recognize that these archetypes provide guidance and are open to personal interpretation, allowing individuals to find their unique path to wellbeing and success.

Transcending the ego refers to a process of moving beyond the limited identification with the self and the patterns of thoughts, beliefs, and desires associated with it.

It involves recognizing the ego as a construct and cultivating a deeper sense of awareness and connection with the larger reality beyond the individual self.

Here's what it means and how it can benefit a person's life:

1. Expanded Consciousness: Transcending the ego allows individuals to tap into a broader and more expansive state of consciousness. It enables them to experience a sense of unity and interconnectedness with others and the world around them. This expanded consciousness can bring about a greater understanding of the interconnected nature of life and foster a deep sense of belonging.

2. Reduced Suffering: The ego often brings about suffering through attachment to desires, fears, and a rigid sense of identity. By transcending the ego, individuals can loosen their grip on these attachments, leading to a reduction in suffering. They become less identified with the fluctuations of the ego and gain a greater sense of inner peace and equanimity.

3. Enhanced Empathy and Compassion: Transcending the ego fosters the development of empathy and compassion. By moving beyond self-centred concerns and recognizing the shared humanity with others, individuals can cultivate a genuine concern for the wellbeing of others. This shift in perspective allows for deeper connections and more harmonious relationships.

4. Increased Clarity and Insight: When the ego is transcended, individuals gain access to a deeper well of wisdom and insight. They become more attuned to their intuition and inner guidance, allowing them to make wiser decisions and navigate life's challenges with greater clarity. Transcending the ego opens up space for creative and innovative thinking.

5. Freedom from Limiting Beliefs: The ego is often associated with limiting beliefs and self-imposed boundaries. By transcending the ego, individuals can break free from these limitations and expand their potential. They become more open to new possibilities, embrace personal growth, and are willing to step outside their comfort zones.

6. Alignment with Higher Purpose: Transcending the ego can lead to a greater alignment with one's higher purpose or a sense of calling. As individuals detach from ego-driven motives and tune into a deeper sense of meaning, they can discover and pursue their passions, contributing to a sense of fulfilment and a meaningful life.

7. Enhanced Wellbeing and Contentment: Ultimately, transcending the ego can bring about a greater sense of wellbeing and contentment. By shifting the focus away from self-centred desires and external validations, individuals can find a more stable and lasting source of happiness within themselves. They experience a sense of inner harmony, irrespective of external circumstances.

How do these work in modern life?

Once we have an understanding of the structure of our mind, we can think about how we are going to best make use of our superego in daily life.

In life

Success can be found by self-awareness (which includes self-knowledge); understanding what you want and why – and then looking into how you can realistically achieve this. We'll go into this later.

Breaking down your own psychology – of what you want and why you want it – comes with an understanding of your own personal id, and your superego analysing the rights and wrongs of this, in terms of how it impacts those around you.

Without this 'id to superego' relationship, your ego might reduce you to childish or un-intellectual actions. Not that being childish means all childlike traits are bad, but we're assuming that adults should progress beyond the urges and non-consequential thinking of a child.

This is not only looking at the theory of 'how you will achieve the success that you want', it's about how you act every day, in your interactions with other people and 'the world' – which includes what you consume from the news, in the media, around you.

Using your superego means calmly analysing each interaction, each situation, looking at why people are acting as they are acting, and how you may best respond to find success.

This is in contrast to the ego, which would cause you to only think of how you can quickly 'get what you want' out of the situation, or 'what this means for me' at any given moment, or essentially uncontrolled reactions and urges that you do not put any thought into, instead purely basing them on either 'I liked that' or 'I did not like that'.

Doing this allows you to remove yourself from simply having immediate reactions to situations, taking more time to find your true innate thought.

This ability to take a moment (or longer) for consideration lets you plan your reaction – or possibly inaction – which can lead to a less anxiety-causing consequence.

Removing your ego in a work situation can be a great thing to do – it's essentially taking the high road of any situation, looking long-term and removing your more childish emotions from the situation.

Everyone knows those people who, in life and therefore at work, are self-centred, looking to achieve a promotion (more power and money) however they can, even if it means doing so in uncivilised ways.

One assumption might be that people who are incredibly self-centred arebeing their most selves, because they don't seem to be bothered by hurting others or how their reputation develops in the long-term. Yet, I've often observed that these people simply live with another kind of ego-based concern that they need the world to see them as clever and powerful.

Meanwhile, human nature ensures that some people (or most/all in certain societies) in the 'boss' position are prone to allowing their ego to control their actions, thoughts and take centre stage, because so many of their ego-based actions can result in a positive reinforcement that pleases their id. This can be simply represented by 'manager jokes'.

So very many times in my life have I seen people in the boss position make unfunny jokes that cause the staff to laugh with energetic gusto, and so they believe they are funny. I have lived/worked in societies where this is especially distinct, where the underlings will do pretty much anything to please the ego of their boss.

I have seen people try to appear what is seen as 'good' by society, yet in reality be completely the opposite behind closed doors. This isn't blaming them for doing so, it's just the way it is, and the way for them to achieve more money to use in life.

Being in a position of power can lead a person to feed their ego, without any higher figure or some form of boundary reminding them that their ego is growing out of control.

In the workplace environment, removing your ego does contain risks. You can see it in the same way as fear – as intelligent people, we understand that fear itself is a weakness and can stop us from achieving. Yet on the other hand, fear can be wise, because it keeps us safe.

Your ego can perform a similar function – the weaknesses it presents can hold you back in terms of evolution and development and happiness, yet, it can be a protective tool or defensive weapon when faced by the ego of others.

While the boss can enjoy having their ego fed by the idea that they are always right, this simply breeds resentment as the staff see that their leader thinks 'I pay, I say', and just because essentially one is in control of the other's livelihood, their word is final.

So, although I've advocated for the removal of ego above, the workplace setting is one where it may be more useful to have awareness of the ego. We've all experienced the moment when someone else questions the thing you've produced, or gets involved in a project that is 'yours', or says something passive-aggressive.

It's very rarely helpful to have an ego-based response in that situation, no matter how difficult it can be for a moment to swallow your pride and be your 'best self' in a constructive and magnanimous response.

However, being the most you doesn't mean thinking that everyone else is annoying and wrong all the time. In an ideal world, removing your ego from the situation of work allows you to remove stress and anxiety over 'what this means for me now' (although this is not always possible due to hard financial realities).

Moreover, if you are someone for whom concern crops up, then a difficult situation or interaction with a colleague might be exactly the thing that you start to think about just as it's bedtime.

This doesn't mean that we're resigned to putting ourselves in a position of weakness every time a conflict arises at work. But to aim towards finding the true instinct from within means making a decision.

Yes, the high road decision is often the most difficult to take, especially when we're faced with either a stupid person (actually, they do exist) who makes us feel impatient or an annoying person who seems to be getting in our way for no reason (AKA being a jobsworth).

The high road decision (being a team player, thanking others for their feedback and opinion etc.) doesn't provide the ego with the primal bolt of adrenaline in the moment, but it usually results in less post-event concern.

Again, in an ideal situation, your manager/boss will see your team-based, ego-less actions and reward them. If that's not where you are then you might need to invest in a 'how to change your job' book.

As a leader, it's a much simpler case. It is vital to remove ego from your actions, as the organisation is a collective group entity and therefore everyone's needs must be seen as equal, alongside the needs of the group as a whole.

Put simply, never assume your jokes are as funny as they seem to be.

In parenting

In some places in the world, it is common to heap praise and idealisation onto what is usually the only child of the family.

The results of how this manifests itself into adult society are glaringly obvious. Google any definition of narcissism and you can find that a cause of believing oneself to be inherently superior to others is often a result of an upbringing where this was reinforced.

On the other side, criticising a child can obviously have a healthy and very unhealthy side to it. Keeping your child

101

grounded is good, but praising them is also good. Ah, parenting. What we can focus on in this case (relevant to ego) is a particular interaction between parent and child.

This has been my experience with parenting. See what you think.

In terms of good parenting and in the closeness of the relationship between a parent and a child, I think there is an important place for the child to be able to mock the parent. I let my children say rude words. I let them call me rude words if it's funny. (in times of mirth they have called me both Dicholas Withycombe and Nick the Dick)

I don't let them have a bad attitude to me, they knew from a young age that 'answering back rudely' was never allowed. Not simply because 'I am the parent and I must be obeyed' nor because I have some kind of ordained greater importance or standing over them, but because it's the right thing to do.

I treat them with respect by making their lives as comfortable as I can, and they return respect by being aware of this and by being nice to me. Less evolved societies see the parent continually reminding the child that they 'owe' the parent back for the work the parent has done, which is not the case with my parenting. I didn't say they 'must respect' me, but they do it by being nice to me.

So, even though they can't and won't simply 'be rude', if we are joking with each other then why can't they call me a dickhead? Because my ego can't take it as I am such an important figurehead of the family? Because other people don't like rude words?

This is simply one example, that knowledge of swear words is the same as other topics: if it is going to be experienced, then it's best done in a place of safety and understanding, e.g. the family or the home.

So, good parenting comes from removing your ego from any situation. Of course there is a time for saying 'you have to do this because I give you life, food and shelter', as long as, at some other time, you have clearly explained your motives: it is your responsibility to raise them to be someone who can cope with the world as a sane and organised adult.

Your child will be resentful if they feel that you simply 'say your way must be done' without providing clarity: that your instruction doesn't come from your ego or love of discipline, but your responsibility. Removing the ego also means having the ability to explain this dynamic without emotion, when usually emotions are spiked by the things children do.

It is a difficult balance, but as well as being the authority figure because you have the responsibility, the fuller life experience so far and the will to help them, you must also sometimes be not 'higher up'. Being on the same level as your child and living in the moment – if only in temporary beats such as when playing a game together – has benefits to being the most you.

Removing your ego also works to give your child the freedom to have their own identity. In these structures, Freud mentions his Oedipus theory, as he always seemed to. I don't believe the Oedipus theory has to be so strict or prescribed – Freud's theory came during a time of parenting in the 1800s and does not relate to the modern civilised world.

Instead, I think that it is relevant to potential resentment of the father figure. This can happen if the father figure restricts the child's own identity: he basically has an idea that 'my child will be like me', and his ego is then hurt when the child is inevitably different and unique. The father can't comprehend why their child is different, and reduces communication, increases criticism and wonders why he is not seen as a King in not only his family but in wider society. This goes into the inevitable development of the crumbling male psyche, which we will talk about later on.

In any situation where you are wondering how to respond

There is a part of more evolved societies that says action is good. If there is a problem then a solution is an action, so let's take an action and that can help. People who are more civilised can sometimes fall into the trap of assuming that all parties are equally as civilised.

The problem there is that taking action can mean 'showing your cards', it can mean making yourself vulnerable. Being vulnerable is unwise if the other party is an a**hole.

Taking action is not always your solution.

Identify when you are being primal and try to move beyond it

The ego responds to the id being based on more primal urges. While the id is seen as solely primal, it's the urge itself that is primal.

It's primal to want to eat, but the act of eating does not have to be primal, although the way some people do it can be uncouth – yes, I said uncouth – and sometimes I have the feeling that personally I'd prefer to eat in a single dining cubicle so that people didn't ask me a question while I have a mouthful of food. But I digress.

Not being egotistical is clearly good for society – but it's the continued internal conversation between the building blocks of your mind that can discover the most you. Being the most you doesn't mean having some kind of zen-clear mind, nor having a world-dominating will to be superior to others.

Being the most you doesn't mean always being successful. It's not even about setting oneself that standard.

Classically, talking to oneself has been signposted as a state of insanity. I'm here to encourage internal conversation as a route to dissecting and analysing stress and anxiety rather than having an expectation that you can combat it, or shout "leave now, and never come back!". If Smeagol had instead gained the confidence to frankly converse with Gollum then he might be enjoying Greenwood forest, rather than have plummeted into the lavas of Mordor.

The idea of using your superego means not thinking about 'what this means for me now' or 'how did I look in that situation', but asking yourself how much you even care about it, and whether the issue is relevant in the wider scheme of time and space.

Gut-Brain-Psychology

So with the gut-brain aspect of things, how does this work in the context of recognised psychological understanding?

In the realm of modern psychology, several alternative theories have emerged that offer different perspectives on understanding the psyche. Here are some notable examples:

1. Cognitive-Behavioral Theory (CBT): CBT focuses on the role of conscious thoughts, beliefs, and behaviours in shaping human experience. It talks about how individuals interpret and make meaning of their experiences, and how these interpretations influence emotions and behaviour. CBT seeks to identify and modify dysfunctional thought patterns and behaviours to improve psychological wellbeing.

2. Humanistic Psychology: Humanistic psychology, represented by theorists such as Carl Rogers and Abraham Maslow, goes for self-actualization, personal growth, and the inherent goodness of individuals. It focuses on understanding human experiences from the perspective of the person, emphasising subjective experiences, self-awareness, and the importance of fulfilling one's potential.

3. Positive Psychology: Positive psychology explores factors that contribute to human flourishing, wellbeing, and optimal functioning. It examines

positive emotions, character strengths, resilience, gratitude, and other factors that promote psychological wellbeing. Positive psychology seeks to understand the conditions that lead to a fulfilling and meaningful life.

4. Attachment Theory: As mentioned, attachment theory, developed by John Bowlby and expanded upon by Mary Ainsworth, examines the nature of attachment bonds between individuals, particularly in early childhood. It highlights the impact of early relationships on psychological development, emotional regulation, and interpersonal relationships throughout the lifespan.

5. Social Cognitive Theory: Social cognitive theory, proposed by Albert Bandura, chooses the reciprocal relationship between behaviour, cognition, and the environment. It focuses on how individuals learn through observation, modelling, and the influence of social factors. The theory highlights the role of self-efficacy beliefs in motivating and guiding behaviour.

6. Evolutionary Psychology: Evolutionary psychology explores the influence of evolutionary processes on human cognition, behaviour, and emotions. It suggests that many psychological traits and behaviours can be understood as adaptations shaped by natural selection. This perspective examines how human psychology has evolved to meet the challenges and demands of the environment.

7. Narrative Psychology: Narrative psychology emphasises the role of stories and narratives in constructing and understanding the self. It explores how individuals make sense of their experiences by creating narratives that give meaning and coherence to their lives. Narrative approaches focus on understanding the stories people tell about themselves

and how these narratives shape their identity and wellbeing.

I find the whole Maslow thing a bit too easy. It seems to be something that's easily quotable but not actually lived: as in an individual person is unlikely to 'move' through the triangle's steps (it's not a pyramid, it's a triangle).

Other people have also commented that it's a bit too conformist for reality:

1. Lack of Empirical Support: Critics argue that Maslow's theory lacks strong empirical evidence to support its hierarchical structure and the specific needs outlined. Some researchers have found limited empirical support for the distinct levels of needs and their sequential nature.

2. Cultural and Individual Variations: Maslow's theory is primarily based on the experiences and values of individuals from Western cultures. Critics argue that the hierarchy of needs may not be universally applicable and that cultural and individual differences should be considered when understanding human motivation and development.

3. Overemphasis on Self-Actualization: Maslow's theory places significant emphasis on self-actualization as the ultimate goal of human development. Critics argue that this focus may be too individualistic and neglect the importance of social and collective wellbeing. They suggest that a broader perspective should be adopted to consider the interconnectedness of individuals within their social and cultural contexts.

4. Lack of Clear Definition and Measurement: Critics argue that Maslow's theory lacks precise definitions and clear measurement criteria for concepts such as self-actualization. This lack of clarity makes it

challenging to test and validate the theory using rigorous scientific methods.

5. Neglect of Negative Motivations: Maslow's theory predominantly focuses on positive motivations and the pursuit of personal growth. Critics argue that it neglects the influence of negative motivations, such as fear, insecurity, and survival instincts, which can significantly impact human behaviour and decision-making.

6. Oversimplification of Human Needs: Critics contend that Maslow's theory oversimplifies the complex nature of human needs by reducing them to a hierarchical structure. Human needs are multidimensional and can vary in their intensity, interdependence, and cultural context, which may not align with Maslow's framework.

7. Lack of Developmental Perspective: Maslow's theory tends to portray self-actualization as an endpoint rather than recognizing the ongoing nature of human development. Critics argue that personal growth and self-actualization can be continuous processes throughout a person's life and should not be seen as a fixed endpoint.

On the theory of Social Cognitive Theory, developed by Albert Bandura, we look at another hypothesised psychological framework that talks about the reciprocal interaction between an individual's behaviour, cognitive processes, and the social environment.

It highlights the role of observational learning, self-efficacy beliefs, and self-regulation in shaping human behaviour and development.

Here are some key aspects of Social Cognitive Theory:

1. Observational Learning: Observational learning, also known as modelling or vicarious learning, suggests that individuals can acquire new behaviours and skills by observing others. Through the process of attention, retention, reproduction, and motivation, individuals learn from models and imitate their behaviour. Observational learning allows individuals to acquire new knowledge and skills without directly experiencing the consequences of their actions.

2. Self-Efficacy: Self-efficacy refers to an individual's belief in their own ability to succeed in specific tasks or situations. Bandura proposed that self-efficacy plays a central role in motivation, behaviour, and achievement. Individuals with high self-efficacy are more likely to set challenging goals, persevere in the face of obstacles, and have a greater sense of control over their actions. Self-efficacy beliefs are influenced by personal experiences, social persuasion, and one's interpretation of physiological and emotional states.

3. Triadic Reciprocal Causation: Social Cognitive Theory goes on about the reciprocal interaction between personal factors, behaviour, and the environment. It suggests that behaviour is influenced by the individual's cognitive processes, such as beliefs, thoughts, and self-perceptions, as well as external factors such as social norms, cultural influences, and situational contexts. This reciprocal causation implies that individuals both shape and are shaped by their environment.

4. Self-Regulation: Self-regulation refers to the process through which individuals set goals, monitor their progress, and adjust their behaviour to achieve desired outcomes. It involves the ability to control one's thoughts, emotions, and actions to align with personal standards and societal expectations. Self-regulation encompasses various processes, including self-

monitoring, self-evaluation, self-reinforcement, and self-punishment.

5. Outcome Expectations: Social Cognitive Theory suggests that individuals are motivated to engage in specific behaviours based on their expectations about the outcomes or consequences of those behaviours. Positive outcome expectations, such as rewards or positive social feedback, can increase the likelihood of engaging in certain behaviours, while negative outcome expectations can deter individuals from engaging in them.

How can you be in control of your gut in a conflicted and controlling world?

Method One: Don't Believe Everything You Hear

I really, really like Jim Carrey.

I admire him, I appreciate him; his existence and his will to exert his energy to make people feel good are both glorious things.

That aside, his personal views on manifesting what you want are well recorded in his various TV interviews. His whole belief system apparently centres on his experience as a boy: he wanted a bicycle very, very much. A couple of days later, a new bicycle was outside his house. His friend had entered him into a competition at a local store and he had won the bike. Therefore, according to Jim Carrey, the correlation was clear.

However, it can be assumed that most young boys really want a bicycle. So that part is a given. The second part simply exists. Some boy - who likely didn't have a bike - had to win that bike. And, there's also a chance that either Jim Carrey subconsciously 'saw' the competition poster in his peripheral vision or what-not (watch Derren Brown if you haven't) or overheard about it in his town, and that further triggered his bike desires. But that not being important: he was simply a boy that won a bike.

That occurrence doesn't logically mean that wishing for things gets things.

It sounds nice, doesn't it? 'I have the power to dream up things and 'the Universe' just sort of 'gifts' them to me because I'm such a natural - and magical - being of said Universe'?

It's very 'first-world person on Instagram' kind of idea-having.

It's arrogant because it directly infers that poor, starving people in the world either could 'manifest' food if they really wanted it enough, or that they lack the necessary magic to make it happen.

The issue is that it may create a situation in which people believe this is all very possible, and then feel frustrated when - for some reason - it doesn't work.

Instead, what if you look at a reality of success – time and patience. Without massive luck, any success needs planning.

Liza Minnelli was promoting something on TV, and she said "when luck meets preparation, magic happens."

I do prefer the body of work from Jim Carrey rather than Liza, but, this is a great piece of advice when planning your life – which sounds so simple yet few people do it. Perhaps they almost think that it's 'cheating'?

Maybe it seems too easy so it's not worth doing? Maybe they lack the patience? In the world of alleged instant success, a decade can seem like a lifetime to get what you want. Yet, a decade is a realistic time zone for planning success in your life. If you'd planned success a decade ago, you'd be there by now.

I've also found that the simple concept of big picture thinking gets more praise than it deserves – such as when an action is discussed and people say, usually with pride; 'but let's think big'. Yes, that's not difficult – of course having a big picture is good, but it is equally useless without the actions that can get there. How can you define the many, many small steps it will take to get to the goal?

So instead of 'think big', if we simply add 'think big and work back', we can see a reality begin to form – the literal (well, metaphorical) steps it takes to get there.

These points are relevant to a joke about a man who prays and prays to God above to win the lottery. He does all the things he's supposed to, but he never wins. He's close to giving up and drops to his knees to finally beg God "why haven't I won the lottery?". At long last, the divine hears him. The clouds part, God appears, and says: "can you at least meet me halfway and buy a ticket?"

At this point, I suppose I should say that if you believe in one of the world deities, then you can just pray for things and I wish you all the best with that particular angle.

Instead of the airy quackery of manifesting, fall back to simpler, time-honoured phrases as keys to life: opportunism.

Opportunity is the luck part of luck meeting preparation. It doesn't sound especially magical and I wouldn't point your anus at it, but simple 'opportunism' means being as prepared as can be, and learning the 'power' of when to spot opportunities.

It means not wasting energy trying to force things – which goes against many modern theories of being successful by being annoyingly pushy (or worse, that simple consistency will result in success, it doesn't) – but identifying where your potential successes actually lie.

Never put yourself in a position of submissiveness by saying that you can achieve something 'one day'. Think big and work back, be patient, prepare and wait for the right opportunities.

Method Two: Actually Go With Your Gut

I mean, definitely test it a few times. Notice the gut feel and see if it was right. I can't say 'definitely always go with your gut', because what if you are a very stupid person? I have no way of knowing that.

But anecdotally, people seem to look back at erroneous decisions and realise that they did have an alternate gut feel that they ignored, because society had brainwashed them into thinking that it's OK to fail. The general message is that 'when we fail we learn'.

Yet, the thing is that when we succeed, we also learn. And, failure very much depends on context. Failing an exam might not be very bad if you get to retake it, for example. If a mountain climber 'fails' to not fall down a mountain then it's really not OK, no matter how much she or he 'learns' on the way down.

It's just nonsense 'success branding' where the ego of people sees them have an urge to look like maverick risk takers who, yes, definitely took risks, but you know what? They paid off and now they are a happy sexy millionaire. It's not that SOME people have to be millionaires, it's that THEY are now a millionaire, and so they can give life advice and shit.

The reality is that you can individually weigh the likelihood of failure and its potential consequences.

We have no way of knowing if the alleged 'risks' taken by others were really risks. If they had someone paying for their rent and food, or they didn't have a responsibility like a child, then they could try and fail.

Obviously it doesn't mean 'never try', despite what Homer said.

But the phrase that survived time is 'go with your gut', not 'go with what people made it look like they achieved on social media'.

Method Three: Eat Fibre (If You Want)

Health advice is just dull and eating fibre doesn't sound as cool as 'manifesting' things with your magical exoticism.

But a healthy gut means a healthy gut-brain axis.

Here are some simple foods that can give you a healthy gut:

1. Garlic: Known for its prebiotic properties, supporting the growth of beneficial bacteria.

2. Onions: Contain prebiotics that nourish the gut microbiome.

3. Leeks: High in prebiotics and a good source of fibre.

4. Asparagus: Provides prebiotics and supports digestive health.

5. Jerusalem artichokes: Rich in prebiotics that aid in gut health.

6. Bananas: Contain prebiotics and are easy to digest.

7. Berries: Packed with fibre and antioxidants to support a healthy gut.

8. Apples: High in fibre and contain pectin, a prebiotic fibre.

9. Oats: A good source of soluble fibre that promotes healthy digestion.

10. Almonds: Provide fibre and healthy fats that promote a balanced gut.

11. Ginger: Known for its anti-inflammatory properties and digestive benefits.

12. Turmeric: Contains curcumin, which can reduce inflammation and support gut health.

13. Yoghurt: Contains probiotics that support a healthy gut microbiome.

14. Sauerkraut: Fermented cabbage that provides probiotics and fibre.

Here are some more that often show up in lists. They seem more esoteric and cool and fun, yet, the above list is just as good.

1. Kefir: A fermented milk drink packed with probiotics and beneficial yeast.

2. Kimchi: A Korean fermented dish made with vegetables and spices.

3. Kombucha: A fermented tea rich in probiotics and antioxidants.

4. Miso: A fermented soybean paste that promotes gut health.

5. Tempeh: A fermented soy product that offers probiotics and fibre.

6. Flaxseeds: Rich in fibre and omega-3 fatty acids, supporting gut health.

Really, you are good with list one though.

Method Four: Reverse-engineering Intuition

So, *manifesting* is silly make-believe because otherwise more people could get what they want.

But, sometimes things seems too coincidental to be anything other than destiny/synchronicity/fate/magic.

What sometimes happens:

1. You have a thought, perhaps you suddenly thought of someone random or a random situation.

2. You then bump into the person somewhere, or the situation occurs.

3. You wonder: is it coincidence or 'something else'?

What if instead of focusing on part 2, you focused on part 1 by listening to yourself more? I understand that we can't permanently listen to each and every one of our brain's various 'what ifs'. Yet, if there is a realisation that 1-to-2 sometimes happens, we can consider that our brains can calculate more than we consciously know.

What this means is that, for example, your brain is doing unbelievably complex things in your body that you don't even think about. It is performing digestion; you couldn't 'think' your way through breaking down an item of food into its constituent parts and then ensuring that those healthy bits travel round your body and feed your various organs while the bad bits get pooed out. You'd have no idea where to begin!

This is one tiny example of all the things your brain-body does. What if you had to 'think' your way through each breath oxygenating your blood and so on and so on?

There's something similar in plants and animals, in terms of they take cues without 'thinking' about it in their mind.

Plants, flowers, and some animals possess various mechanisms that allow them to sense and respond to changes in weather conditions. While they may not have the same level of consciousness or awareness as humans do, they have evolved physiological and behavioural adaptations that enable them to detect and react to environmental cues. Here are some ways they perceive weather changes:

1. Light cues: Plants have photoreceptors that detect changes in light patterns and use this information to adjust their growth and development. For example, changes in day length (photoperiod) signal the changing seasons and trigger flowering in many plants.

2. Temperature cues: Temperature variations serve as critical signals for both plants and animals. Plants can sense temperature changes through temperature receptors in their cells. Certain temperature thresholds trigger specific responses, such as seed germination, leaf budding, or the onset of dormancy.

3. Moisture cues: Plants have specialised cells that can sense changes in moisture levels. They respond to

fluctuations in humidity and soil moisture, adjusting their water intake and closing their stomata (tiny pores on leaves) to prevent excessive water loss during dry periods.

4. Atmospheric pressure cues: Some animals, especially birds, can sense changes in atmospheric pressure. They use this ability to anticipate weather changes, particularly during migratory journeys. For example, they can detect approaching storms or changes in air pressure associated with a weather system.

5. Chemical cues: Some plants release volatile compounds into the air in response to specific weather conditions. For instance, certain plants emit fragrant compounds before rainfall, which may attract pollinators. Additionally, changes in humidity and temperature can alter the scent of flowers, affecting their attractiveness to pollinators.

These responses are often innate and instinctual, driven by genetic programming and evolutionary adaptations. They aren't listening in to the weather report. Probably.

So, what if, instead of magic things and destiny, part of your brain could take nanoscopic hints and tips and cues from things that you couldn't even 'think' about, and then tell you that, in all likelihood, Sarah from your primary school whom you haven't seen for 25 years is going to be in the supermarket next week?

So you have that thought and then wouldn't you know it, you see Sarah shopping for flax seeds in aisle 9.

Sometimes these thoughts are louder than others. Write them down? I can't willingly advocate 'journaling' but you could keep a brain record so that at least you have proof that your intuition is working for you; and then think about the kind of reaction you have (AKA person you want to be) if the situation was to actually occur.

PART FOUR
YOUR GENITALS

Your Genitals

Most self-development books, or let's face it most books in existence do not directly refer to their reader's genitals.

The reason I have is because they are important. Now, of course that's quite funny, but also true.

Sometimes, psychology referred to the genitals - Freud (1856-1939) couldn't help but refer to the penis on many occasions - but most modern books talk about the mind, about learning, thinking, meditating and so on. Modern society says that you should get the Calm app and use a habit tracker to ensure you drink enough water throughout the day. Now those two things are indeed mentally healthy but so is sex.

As usual, being human, we over-complicate and over-think sex. Not a fault, nothing to lament, but how can we possibly look at the 'whole person' without staring at their genitals? Let's take a long, lingering look at yours.

We can't look at your family jewels without seeing them through the lens of Freud.

Freud, known as the father of psychoanalysis, extensively studied human sexuality and its psychological implications.

He proposed that sexual instincts were a fundamental driving force in human behaviour. Freud introduced the concept of the Oedipus complex, suggesting that children develop unconscious sexual desires for their opposite-sex parent and view their same-sex parent as a rival. He also highlighted the role of unconscious desires and conflicts in shaping one's sexual experiences.

According to Freud, human behaviour and experiences are influenced by unconscious drives and conflicts that stem from early childhood experiences.

He believed that sexual instincts, known as libido, were a fundamental driving force in human behaviour. Freud divided the human psyche into three parts: the id, ego, and superego.

As briefly covered before: the id represents the primitive, unconscious part of the mind that operates on the pleasure principle, seeking immediate gratification of instinctual desires. It is primarily driven by sexual and aggressive instincts.

The ego, on the other hand, operates on the reality principle and serves as the conscious mediator between the id and the external world. It tries to find realistic ways to satisfy the id's desires while taking into account social norms and consequences.

Freud argued that conflicts arise between the id and the ego, as societal rules and restrictions often clash with the instinctual desires of the id. These conflicts can manifest in various ways within an individual's sexual experiences. For example, certain sexual desires may be repressed or pushed into the unconscious due to societal taboos or personal guilt. Freud referred to this phenomenon as the "repression" of sexual impulses.

According to Freud, repressed sexual desires and conflicts can find expression through various mechanisms, including dreams, slips of the tongue (known as Freudian slips), and parapraxes (errors in behaviour). These manifestations can provide insights into an individual's unconscious sexual desires and conflicts.

Furthermore, Freud introduced the concept of psychosexual development, which describes the progression of sexual instincts and experiences from infancy to adulthood.

He proposed that childhood experiences and conflicts, particularly those related to the parent-child relationship, significantly influence an individual's sexual development.

Freud's theory of psychoanalysis suggested that unresolved conflicts or traumas from childhood, such as unresolved Oedipal or Electra complex issues, could shape an individual's sexual experiences and desires in adulthood. For example, unresolved conflicts related to parental figures might contribute to difficulties in forming and maintaining intimate relationships or lead to specific sexual preferences or dysfunctions.

Freud's concept of sexual repression revolves around the idea that society imposes restrictions and prohibitions on sexual desires, leading to the suppression of those desires in the individual's mind.

Freud argued that sexual repression occurs primarily due to societal norms, moral values, and cultural expectations that dictate what is considered acceptable or taboo in terms of sexual expression.

According to Freud, sexual repression operates through a process called sublimation, where socially unacceptable sexual desires are redirected or transformed into socially acceptable forms of behaviour. This process allows individuals to express their repressed sexual energy through other means, such as artistic creativity, intellectual pursuits, or productive work.

Freud believed that sexual repression has profound effects on an individual's psychological wellbeing. The repressed sexual energy can give rise to psychological conflicts, neurotic symptoms, and various forms of psychopathology. Freud argued that repressed sexual desires and conflicts could manifest as symptoms such as anxiety, depression, obsessions, or sexual dysfunctions.

In Freud's psychoanalytic theory, the unconscious mind plays a crucial role in the process of sexual repression.

He proposed that repressed sexual desires are pushed into the unconscious, where they continue to exert influence on an individual's thoughts, feelings, and behaviours. These repressed desires can emerge in various ways, such as in dreams, slips of the tongue, or in the form of symbolic representations.

Freud also introduced the concept of defence mechanisms, which are psychological strategies used by the ego to cope with conflicts and anxiety arising from repressed sexual desires. Defence mechanisms, such as repression, denial, or rationalisation, serve to keep the unconscious desires hidden from conscious awareness.

However, these defence mechanisms can result in the distortion of reality and hinder personal growth and self-understanding.

Michel Foucault

A person of note, after Freud, was Michel Foucault (1926-1984). Foucault, a French philosopher and social theorist, explored the intersection of power, knowledge, and sexuality. He argued that sexuality was not solely an innate biological aspect but rather a product of historical, cultural, and social constructs. Foucault introduced the concept of "biopower," which examines how power is exercised over individuals' bodies and sexualities, particularly through social institutions and norms.

Biopower refers to the techniques and strategies employed by institutions and systems of governance to manage and control populations at a biological and social level.

Foucault's concept of biopower challenges the traditional understanding of power as a purely repressive force. Instead, he argues that power operates through productive and regulatory mechanisms, shaping and directing the behaviours and experiences of individuals.

Biopower focuses on the intersection of power, knowledge, and bodies, particularly in the context of modern societies.

According to Foucault, biopower involves two interrelated processes:

Anatomopolitics: This refers to the regulation and control of individual bodies, often through disciplinary institutions such as hospitals, schools, and prisons. Anatomopolitics seeks to manage and normalise bodies, imposing norms and standards of behaviour, health, and sexuality. It operates through techniques such as medical examinations, surveillance, and the categorization and classification of individuals based on biological or medical criteria.

Biopolitics: Biopolitics extends beyond the individual body to encompass the management and control of populations as a whole. It focuses on the regulation of life processes, including birth rates, mortality rates, health, and public hygiene. Biopolitics involves the use of statistical analysis, social policies, and government interventions to optimise the health and wellbeing of the population, often in the name of public health or national interests.

Foucault argues that biopower operates through a range of mechanisms, including disciplinary practices, regulatory measures, and the production of knowledge about bodies and populations. These mechanisms work to shape and govern the behaviours, practices, and experiences of individuals, often subtly and on a collective level.

Esther Perel

Going on chronologically, we move to Esther Perel (born 1958). Esther Perel is a Belgian psychotherapist and author who has made significant contributions to the understanding of desire, intimacy, and infidelity in modern relationships. She explores the complexities and challenges that individuals face in maintaining passion and connection within long-term partnerships. Perel's work has gained widespread recognition for its unique and thought-provoking insights into contemporary relationships.

Perel's notable works and ideas include:

"Mating in Captivity: Unlocking Erotic Intelligence" (2006):

In this book, Perel explores the tension between intimacy and desire within long-term relationships. She argues that the qualities that foster intimacy, such as security, closeness, and emotional connection, can often dampen erotic desire. Perel suggests that cultivating a sense of separateness, maintaining individuality, and fostering mystery can help sustain sexual desire in committed relationships.

Infidelity and the Paradox of Betrayal:

Perel has extensively examined the complex dynamics surrounding infidelity and the ways in which it challenges traditional notions of commitment and monogamy. She explores how individuals can experience infidelity as both a betrayal and an expression of longing, desire, or a quest for aliveness. Perel challenges the black-and-white view of infidelity and encourages a deeper understanding of its underlying motivations.

The Role of Fantasy and Imagination:

Perel goes on about the importance of fantasy and imagination in maintaining desire and eroticism within relationships. She encourages individuals to explore their innermost desires and create a space for erotic play and novelty. Perel believes that embracing imagination and fantasy can reignite passion and curiosity, helping individuals reconnect with their own desires and the desires of their partners.

Perel recognizes the impact of cultural and societal factors on relationships and sexuality. She explores how societal norms, expectations, and pressures can shape individuals' experiences of desire and intimacy. Perel encourages individuals to question societal scripts and redefine their own sexual narratives, free from external expectations and judgments. She emphasises the importance of open communication, vulnerability, and empathy in navigating the complexities of desire, intimacy, and infidelity.

In more modern times, Roxane Gay is an American writer, cultural critic, and professor known for her powerful and insightful works on topics such as feminism, race, body image, and popular culture. Her book "Bad Feminist" (2014) gained significant acclaim and has become a seminal work within contemporary feminist discourse.

In "Bad Feminist," Gay explores the complexities and contradictions of modern feminism while reflecting on her own experiences. The book delves into a wide range of subjects, including politics, literature, media, and popular culture, through the lens of intersectional feminism.

One of the central themes in "Bad Feminist" is the societal pressure for women to conform to certain beauty standards. Gay critiques the expectations placed on women to adhere to narrow and often unattainable ideals of beauty, mentioning the damaging effects of these standards on women's self-esteem and sense of worth. She discusses how the media and popular culture perpetuate and reinforce these standards, leading to body dissatisfaction and the policing of women's appearance.

Her writing challenges the notion that being a feminist means adhering to a perfect set of beliefs or actions. She embraces the concept of being a "bad feminist" as a way to acknowledge her own contradictions and imperfections while still striving for gender equality and social justice. She encourages readers to embrace the complexities of their own identities and experiences, emphasising that it is possible to be critical of societal norms while still finding joy and pleasure within popular culture.

Societal expectations

Here are some general examples of societal expectations and cultural influences on women's appearance that are commonly discussed within feminist discourse:

Body Image and Beauty Standards: Gay addresses the pressure for women to have a specific body type, often emphasising thinness, youthfulness, and specific features. She explores the damaging effects of unrealistic beauty standards perpetuated by the media, fashion industry, and popular culture.

Beauty Rituals and Products: Gay examines the time, effort, and financial resources that women are expected to invest in beauty rituals and products. This includes everything from cosmetics and skincare regimens to hair treatments and body modifications, highlighting the societal expectation that women should prioritise their appearance.

Sexualization and Objectification: She also discusses how women are often objectified and reduced to their physical attributes, leading to the perception that their worth is based on their attractiveness and sexual appeal. Gay explores how this objectification can impact women's self-esteem, relationships, and overall experiences.

Body Policing and Criticism: Gay highlights how women's bodies are often subjected to intense scrutiny and criticism. This can include judgement and shaming based on weight, clothing choices, grooming, and other aspects of appearance. The book examines how this body policing creates a culture of self-consciousness and perpetuates harmful beauty ideals.

Intersectionality and Beauty Standards: Gay acknowledges that beauty standards and expectations can differ based on factors such as race, class, and ability. She explores how societal norms disproportionately impact women from marginalised communities and the importance of recognizing the unique challenges they face.

Sex From The Lens of A Controlling Society

The common phrase 'sex sells' is a truism. Sex is used to push us to buy stuff. Many adverts you see use this basic concept. Buy our product and get sex. Even beyond underwear, jeans, fragrances. Use our wifi router and get closer to someone you fancy and have a relationship.

Activation of Brain Areas: Sexual arousal triggers the activation of specific areas in the brain, including the limbic system, hypothalamus, amygdala, and prefrontal cortex. These regions are involved in emotional processing, reward anticipation, and decision-making.

Release of Neurotransmitters: Sexual arousal leads to the release of neurotransmitters such as dopamine, which plays a crucial role in reward and pleasure pathways. Dopamine release can create feelings of excitement, motivation, and pleasure.

Increased Blood Flow: Arousal triggers increased blood flow to the genital area, leading to physiological changes such as erection in males and vaginal lubrication in females. This increased blood flow is facilitated by the dilation of blood vessels in the genital region.

Activation of the Hypothalamic-Pituitary-Gonadal (HPG) Axis: The HPG axis is responsible for the release of sex hormones. Sexual arousal stimulates the hypothalamus to release gonadotropin-releasing hormone (GnRH), which signals the pituitary gland to release luteinizing hormone (LH) and follicle-stimulating hormone (FSH). LH and FSH, in turn, stimulate the production of sex hormones like testosterone in males and oestrogen in females.

Heightened Sensory Perception: Sexual arousal can enhance sensory perception, making individuals more attuned to stimuli related to the perceived source of arousal. This can involve heightened attention to visual, auditory, and tactile cues associated with sexual stimulation.

Jean Kilbourne

Jean Kilbourne is an American author, speaker, and filmmaker known for her groundbreaking work in examining the impact of advertising on society, particularly in relation to gender, sexuality, and body image. She is widely recognized for her critical analysis of the portrayal of sex in advertising and its influence on cultural norms.

In her influential book "Can't Buy My Love: How Advertising Changes the Way We Think and Feel" (2000), Kilbourne delves into the tactics and effects of advertising, specifically focusing on the use of sexualized imagery to sell products. She argues that advertising often perpetuates harmful beauty standards, objectifies women, and reinforces gender inequalities.

Kilbourne highlights the following key points in her analysis:

Objectification of Women: Kilbourne argues that advertising frequently objectifies women, reducing them to sexual objects and emphasising their physical appearance over their abilities or qualities.

Unrealistic Beauty Standards: She critiques the promotion of unrealistic beauty ideals in advertising, which can lead to body dissatisfaction, low self-esteem, and negative body image among individuals, especially women and girls.

Sexualization of Products: Kilbourne demonstrates how advertisers strategically employ sexualized imagery to make products more appealing and create associations between sex and consumer goods.

Reinforcement of Gender Stereotypes: She examines how advertising perpetuates traditional gender roles and stereotypes, presenting women as passive objects of desire and men as active consumers.

Impact on Relationships: Kilbourne explores the potential impact of sexualized advertising on relationships, arguing that it can contribute to the objectification and commodification of intimate interactions.

Is This Changing?

Now, you might say or see that this is changing, a bit. 'Kind of changing a bit' is where we are now. Some brands will use what they would call non-mainstream people or diverse or inclusive. TV adverts about some products - let's use antiperspirant or body cream as the examples - have models with dyed hair, vast reserves of personal body fat, freckles, impetigo, and down's syndrome. These are not my labels, these are factual descriptions.

Some people might say that showing 'different people' is 'good', for whatever reason they believe this to be good for. But from another angle, it's still bad. Any TV advert showing anyone, by default, glamourises and promotes the thing that it is showing.

All this means is that girls who do not have dyed hair or impetigo may feel bad about themselves. That may sound facetious, but body image can take unexpected and extreme routes. To which the comment 'well brands just can't win then can they?!', TO WHICH my answers would be: they don't have to.

We shouldn't live in a world in which a business should be lauded one way or another. These are simple and functional products. People - you - retain the option of not watching TV adverts, nay, not buying many products. It's also important to notice that some types of product or business will go down this route, while others retain traditional advertising options.

Fragrances and designer clothing businesses, as I write, use models who are taller than the average height and have very little body fat or muscle.

It's as if business as a whole has said 'OK, for daily use stuff, you can look at fats and weirdos. But for example stuff like pricey cars and clothes, it's still going to be thin people with more visible cheekbones aged between 25 and 35'.

That's their hypothetical words, NOT MINE!

Here, we have a choice. Either we believe that businesses and the leaders or decision-makers therein do actually care about anything they say they care about, or, they don't really care and they want to make more profit.

I suppose that there could potentially be the declared situation of them caring but also still very much wanting to make profit, but that just seems like make-believe nonsense. None of the changes of so-called inclusivity happened until it started being pointed out by the people, AKA the 'consumer'.

The word 'consumer' is a word we now see as commonplace but it really reflects the contempt and disgust that businesses have for their customers, as if they see them more as locusts, pigs with snouts relentlessly scoffing in a trough of unnecessary items and plastic.

We do but consume. If they show us what they think we want to see, we will continue to consume. Sex sells will always be true thanks to hormones.

The message now is simply that someone else who is like you - whether portly or brown - is also increasing their social acceptability thanks to the use of our product. Buy our product and you too will be accepted, loved, fucked.

This is the tonality of advertising. Yet it's about even more than the tone. In context of the above authors and the generally accepted situation of sexism in society, we cannot not but look at products outrightly called 'cosmetics' or 'beauty'. The definition of cosmetic is 'affecting only the appearance of something rather than its substance'.

This is used by women. The standard situation in this regard has been that people who use make up say that they do not wear it for others, they wear it for themselves. The debate here is not if that is true, but even if it is, then what is behind the need to smear something on one's face for one's personal need? This is not a criticism, and yes biologically this author is absolutely a man.

But how can we address the topic of sex in the modern world without looking at the topic of so called 'beauty' being achieved by the alteration or adjustment of one's face?

Businesses make lots and lots of money by telling women that their latest product is the best ever product they have ever made. Forget the last 30 years of products that they said were absolutely the best ever. It's only this brand new range of totally new products with a totally new special ingredient that will make you look better. The other products they made in the past only made you look a bit better. If at all. The last one SAID it made you look much younger and fresher and so on, but this NEW one makes you look SO young and fresh that you basically look 5 years old. If that.

That's what they say, not I. And then some women decide that they do want that, so they buy it and use it. Then they throw away the packaging, but it's OK because a percentage of the packaging is recyclable. So then they can post on social media about something to do with sustainability or making positive change.

This is a commentary, not a criticism, remember. And men are not absent from the nonsense: a recently released product for men is called "magnesium defence". This means that if you use "magnesium defence" face moisturiser or shower gel, you are kind of being a tough robocop and you need defending from all the tough things that you do, such as hoisting sails and pulling in fishing nets, fighting bad guys and abseiling walls. Mowing the lawn on a bi-weekly rota and ordering the patatas bravas at the new restaurant in town. Women want you and men want to be you. "Magnesium defence".

Here are just some recent examples but there are thousands upon thousands:

Vodafone: Vodafone has a TV advert wherein a young white man in a wheelchair plays online games with a young black lady and later on, due to Vodafone's network, they start some kind of relationship.

Apple: Apple released a new device that was mainly identically the same as a previous device but they said it's small somehow (thin?) but also 'big'. The final word of the advert is a coquettish female voice saying "big" in a seductive manner.

Renault: Renault had an advert for their Megane with the track *'shakin' that ass'* as the tune, due to the car's apparently big posterior.

Vrbo: The villa rental site Vrbo showed two black lesbians kissing each other in their advert for holiday rentals.

Lotto: The UK national lottery showed a gay kiss between two men.

KFC: KFC UK had an advert when a white girl and her white boyfriend were going to order but the white boyfriend didn't know what to order. The white girl then looked at two black men who had ordered well and she looked at them lustily.

Specsavers: Specsavers have an advert where women of different ages and races talk excitedly about a man who is 'seeing half the town' and will 'pop the question' but then they reveal they are talking about an optician.

Compare the Market: A woman was shown as being very sexually interested in the male meerkat in this advert (which is also an example of sexism as they wouldn't show a man having a girlfriend of a female meerkat)

Bacardi: Also inter-species sexuality with a male cat seductively licking the shoulder of a woman, ditto sexism.

Marks and Spencer: M&S Food "Adventures in Love" Campaign was launched in 2016. The adverts showcased couples enjoying romantic moments while highlighting M&S food products.

Coca Cola: In 2017, Coca-Cola released an ad titled "Pool Boy" as part of their "Taste the Feeling" campaign. The commercial featured a brother and sister competing for the attention of an attractive pool boy. At the end of the ad, it is revealed that the brother was interested in the pool boy.

McCain: In 2019, McCain Foods released an advert titled "Here's To Love," which featured 'diverse' couples, including a same-sex couple, enjoying moments of love and connection.

Some of these operate under the guise of diversity and inclusivity, but the main message is: buy our product, get sex somehow.

The notable thing here is that all of this sexualisation happens outside of interactions with other humans. And, of course, it's made worse by social media. As many things are.

So before you meet another person, you are being told that you need to consume various things to make you fuckable to others. Then you look at more or less anything on your phone and see people showing the most fuckable version of themselves, however they can manage it.

So, when you finally come to meet someone in person, you're already programmed into playing one of the various roles that people on various forms of media are portraying.

This is why it may then leave you feeling cold that no one said your skin looks rejuvenated, or your physique reminds them of Superman.

The projected level of fulfilment portrayed across all media is so high as to be unattainable by many. As humans, we want what is rare. Our brains love the rare because it is rare, so others want it. Who wants something that no one else wants? Yuck! Thus, we are driven to consume things that will get us to the unattainably high levels.

Here's a short anecdote from real life:

I know someone who works as a personal trainer. It is not rare for him to receive salacious messages from female gym-goers, directly asking him to go to their houses for sexual escapades.

It is important to note that this is not about 'shaming' any such women or saying anything about what men or women do. If that was the book, then it would be entirely about the evils of men in the sexual sphere.

The point is that the women who message him are quite happily (so it seems) married. House/car/husband/kids deal.

But they are apparently unfulfilled in some way. The 'desperate housewives' trope is nothing new, but as a trope it is sexist and presumptuous.

If we remove the accusatory and generalised trope, we still see that the fulfilment criteria is beyond the preconceived notion of what should supposedly fulfil. Stability, security, progeny, love, materialism, hobby, freedoms. All insufficient, apparently. It needs a personal trainer sex icon on top as the sexual cherry on top of a middle class life cake.

Remember when Freud talked about repression in the 1800s? I mean, remember when it was previously referenced in this book. We are socially neuro-groomed to think that men are lusty and women aren't. So, we are told it's OK if men are, because they just *are*, and women aren't, so therefore not one of them is allowed to be because that's not what's natural?

In terms of lust, I ask you: Which gender fills entire stadiums with a teenage audience that, literally, SCREAMS toward the opposite-gendered popstar on stage? Yes, girls (not shaming but observing!).

Boys are accepted as just tugging on their todgers willy-nilly, but it's girls who will reach feverish levels of lust toward a young man who is acclaimed to be the most fuckable of his genre. Not blame anywhere here, just commentary. If any blame is to be apportioned then it would be to male society for repressing women, but, still those people what did (and do) the repressing are also faulted humans, so it's difficult to blame anyone. God maybe? No that's ridiculous.

All this, to say sex isn't bad. But never underestimate its power over standard daily activities, choices, benign thoughts. Always be aware of businesses' usage of sex in making to buy stuff you don't even need.

How can you be in control of your genitals in a conflicted and controlling world?

Method One: Awareness Before Action

In health and wellness, we talk about emotion, mindset, mood, mentality, psychology, feelings and so on. Well, if you've enjoyed some form of sexual intercourse, then I hope you agree that it feels great!

We can talk all day about eating fruit, doing exercise, communicating openly and the full set of wellbeing goodness, but an unsatisfying relationship with the topic of sex may cause angst, impatience, sadness, frustration and isolation.

I really need to make it clear at this point that this is a logical, adult discussion. I've brought up this point before (that sex affects mood) and someone replied: "Oh so all a woman needs is a man to make things OK?!"

It may have seemed like a great opportunity to be triggered/indignant, but the actual words I used at that time and am also using now are these: because humans have hormones, sex affects our mood.

I am not 'recommending' anything at all in the world of sex because I am not an expert (I will not write 'sexpert'). Some

136

monks around the world may have purposefully selected celibacy to free themselves from that specific concern of how to obtain sex. I'm not saying do it or don't do it – this is, simply, about awareness.

Awareness and acceptance of how sex can affect us and therefore domino to other people is key to our level of self identity.

Method Two: Listening to your mood (and questioning its validity)

In wellbeing, we're told to tune in to our minds, pause and listen to what it's saying and how we're feeling. This is a great thing to do – but, with acceptance of our moods being swayed by hormones, we can accept that we might be thinking complete rubbish.

Valuing your thoughts is important, but devaluing them can be important too. 'I'm probably being stupid here' is not necessarily a bad thing to think.

No one should be so arrogant that they cannot recognise their own mental nonsense.

This comes into play with your hormones as they have such massive control over you.

Put simply: a build-up of certain hormones caused by a lack of sexual activity (either with someone else or by yourself – or if you're lucky then with perhaps a group of people) can make a person act short-tempered, and/or overly flirtatious, among other things.

It's important to know that in the following words, I am not excusing or saying anyone has the excuse to act in certain ways just because of their hormones. But as a man (I can't speak for female behaviour but I imagine there are similarities because we are all human), you might start to take negative actions if you aren't aware that your hormones are controlling you. This can include sending people salacious messages on social media platforms, and/or acting inappropriately in a professional or other environment.

(again, this is not *excusing* such behaviour in any way at all)

Self-awareness can mean recognising this before you might begin to act inappropriately. It means recognising that you are being short-tempered due to your hormones.

(this is not accusing anyone of being irrational due to hormones, but a personal acceptance that our mood may be affected by hormones)

Getting control of yourself is great. But others may not have done so, and knowing this helps you to understand why some people are in a bad mood, or in changing moods. It doesn't mean that it gives anyone an 'excuse' to act in a certain way. But at least you have an idea of the potential reasons. (though it might not be their hormones. They might just be born assholes. They exist.)

Method Three: Owning Sexiness as positive motivation

'How can I motivate myself to exercise and stay fit?' is a common question in wellbeing. There are usually a bunch of suggestions that revolve around mindset. But sex is relevant. I'll say it. Looking at really sexy people can give you the get-up-and-go that you need to make it to the gym or fling yourself around the room at home.

Being open about reasons for keeping fit is positive. 'I exercise to look good and to therefore increase my chances of physically interacting with someone sexy' is an honest thought. However, I can't help but feel that it's being taken too far in some contexts.

We know it but still can be baited: it's actually unhealthy to look like current social icons. I won't talk about whether it's healthy or not for women to be told by other women on social media to focus quite that much on their bottom size. I won't talk about whether it's healthy for a woman talking about 'not

138

judging yourself' alongside a half-naked photo revealing no fat and the 'perfect' hourglass figure. I won't talk about these things because the world does not need a man talking about women's issues. I will say that it is drastically unhealthy for a man to get the Men's Health cover look with rock hard rippled abs coupling enormous biceps. Being as sexy as Superman or Thor is unrealistic, un-sustainable and unhealthy.

Sex and sexiness are aspects that people need to understand in order to be true to the most you. We've talked about a few of them but it's part of the overall discussion of self. Do you have goals related to your physique? How realistic are they? What happens mentally if you get there – or don't?

What is your relationship with your appearance and clothes? Does it ever cause you concern? Have you ever bought something and didn't consciously realise that sex was promised by the advertising?

Method Four: Assumptions and Repression

Society tells us that monogamy is absolutely good. It tells us that men can rescue women, but it also tells us that women - allegedly the 'best' ones, rescue men. In film circles, it's commonly known as a "manic pixie dream girl."

This term was coined by film critic Nathan Rabin in 2007 to describe a specific type of female character often seen in movies. The manic pixie dream girl is portrayed as whimsical, spontaneous, and free-spirited, with the primary purpose of inspiring the male protagonist and helping him rediscover his passion for life. She is often used as a catalyst for his personal growth and transformation. This serves to reduce complex female characters to mere plot devices for the male protagonist's development.

We are fed this information non-stop, yet we have limits on what we can say ourselves.

Of course, the topic of sex in our current time is more openly discussed versus, let's say Victorian England.

Yet, there are still assumptions, taboos and things that we are told are bad.

There may be things - sexual things - that a particular individual either likes, or might like.

Now, this may sound like a grooming kind of encouragement, but it isn't. The point is that if a person has not come to terms with their own sexual inclinations, then they are repressed. Repression in the mind will always out itself, one way or another. I love the country of Japan, but it could be said that pushing down with God-heavy social pressure to quietly and absolutely conform does result in the squeezing out of some rather bizarre proclivities and desires.

Downplaying sexual desires has been so ingrained in our society - mainly by religion - that while the topic is more openly discussed now, there are many barriers to a person coming to a form of calm awareness and acceptance about their own sexuality. This means sexuality in the form of general persuasions and also finer preferences.

There is not a 'solution' to this, it is not to say that people should just do what they want sexually all the time, as that wouldn't really work, and, consent is paramount (just stating the obvious). What it's about is the downplaying.

Sex as a part of oneself should not be downplayed. 'You are human, ipso facto you want sex, now stop thinking about it any more or you're being bad'. That's the general line of thinking that a lot of people are told.

Without there being an immediate solution - we can't just all sit around talking about sex all day - what we need to do is remove the topic from the realm of subtle advertising and make it a more considered part of social discussion. Maybe like food? Not exactly like food, but not dis-similar from food, in an adults only context.

In the previous century we were more blind to food, whereas now there are very many TV programmes about food. To control urges towards sugar/fat/salt, we talk about food in advertising, sugar and alcohol adverts are restricted, and there are initial discussions on reducing adverts and also special offers on junk food (this is of course taking a long time because people in power really care a lot about money).

People's urges in a sexual context are stirred by advertising and TV programmes - and then they are very much left with their dick in their hands, either figuratively or literally.

I don't know how we get to utopia, but from the context of the most you, all we can do to be our most selves is to recognise how our mood is when we wake and go through the day, how is our outlook on both that day and on life in general? Society says that if it is your situation with sex that defines this - in any way - then you are bad in some way or other.

But this is the society that is also controlling us, wherever it can, through either promoting or restricting the idea of sex.

This book isn't about fixing society, as that isn't possible even if it was globally attempted. There is no simple conclusion to our present state, where some men blame women if they are sexually unfulfilled, and women are told to 'own' their sexuality, and both genders can display their body parts on social media to the world.

We live in a world where the #metoo movement was, obviously, the fault of men. Yet during the moment when the movement had momentum, some people made claims that they were groped years ago by a man. Thereafter, they not only made no further claims but dropped the issue of feminism entirely from their words or output, reverting back to showing their boobs (which is their right) on their social media accounts via carefully curated and edited photos that also showed the socially accepted 'perfect' side of their lives.

It may seem like either simple 'reporting' or even a good and positive 'movement' yet, it is a story told by the media and the rich, successful people who earn their living from the media.

It's a story that stirs emotions related to sexuality in society. But when the story has become less successful in clickbait results, the media - and the rich, successful people in the story - move on to something else. Your emotions and sense of injustice remain, while the protagonists regress to using their looks to get money.

Do not get sucked in. Get sucked off!

Now were you aware that we finished this section with a sex-based joke just so you might think you enjoyed the section?

Good. You've learned something. And learning something gives you 1 socially accepted cache point. When you reach 100 points, you win a handjob. Not really!

PART FIVE
YOU AND LIFE

How to be the most creative you

Understand the urge to create and keep it as something positive.

Creativity is presumptively seen as something positive. It's funny, the more that you think about it. Creativity. Let's get creative. Brainstorming. Thought leadership. Ideation. Guru. Artist. I think the worst one would be 'content creator'. There's something about it ending with the 'o' in creator that really emphasises what nonsense it all is. Yet, all of these things are seen as positive.

Firstly, that's silly. History, now and the future all show us that people can very easily create bad things – either purposefully negative 'creations' or just meaningless pigswill. Many people do it. A man called Simon Sinek has made a career out of tweeting 1,000 variations of 'teamwork makes the dreamwork' and re-telling other people's stories as he dreams of looking like Bruce Springsteen. A man called Adam Grant keeps tweeting and publishing things but, as a reasonably intelligent person, I can't find a clear meaning in any of his thoughts or words. Another man called Steven Bartlett seems to push the idea that, because he has made a small amount of money, he can, nay should give life advice. By his own theory, others who have made more money than him are therefore more worth listening to than he is. And no one misses noticing his part-stifled thrilled smiles when a podcast guest starts crying. Tears are hellaciously click-baity things. And they show he has empathy.

His book is called 'happy sexy millionaire', aiming to tug on the potential reader's genital-strings to make a purchase. Sex sells.

What can we learn from this? That it seems to be men who believe they must apportion wisdom to the masses because their mummy said they are good so they are good? Yes, but also that we must not fetishise mere 'creativity'. And, that I am a man what wrote this book and I also create content. And my

144

mummy said I was good. So, there's some sexiness we have to be comfortable with here. Did I say sexiness? I meant hypocrisy.

But what this is really about is that we must not believe creativity is absolutely good.

The presumptive belief pushes us in a direction of believing that we *should* do it. Further information on this also tells us that we pretty much MUST. Even if we don't actually feel like it. We're told that consistency is key! Going out of our comfort zone is the tits! TikTok everything!

We can turn back to Bruce Springsteen as an example of this: his real genius happened when he was at certain stages of his life; difficult ones. This isn't to say that you can only create when sad, it's saying that in the right moment and a certain mood, you can unleash gold. But at other times, you will put out 'general stuff' that simply can't match your best work.

So how can you keep creativity as something positive, something to enjoy, something that never causes you stress due to feelings of fretful obligation?

1.   Only do it if it comes naturally

Since people realised they could make money off of it, the corporate world tractor-beamed creativity into its ugly and mechanical alien ship. This means that people who work in incredibly ordinary and boring jobs have 'some say' in creativity. Fashion businesses (AKA 'brands) pay 'creators' to do stuff for them so they can sell more random tat to people who really have nothing inside. Marketing teams are told to 'get creative' but only if it is in absolute compliance with a *brand's* 50-page design guidelines and won't offend any human on planet Earth. This means that people today find it completely rational to say that you must find that special place in your brain to 'get creative', but then put its expressions into a Trello board or another equally vile piece of organisational software.

Instead, look at it this way: what globally famous piece of historical art was ever produced this way? Did Da Vinci have a target demographic in mind? No. Any fantastic thing you can think of, whether a painting, film, book or thought, was borne forth at will. This doesn't mean that if it's not of legendary quality you shouldn't bother, it means: you need certain time, space and moments for the truth to simmer and then boil over from within.

A simple way of sounding this out in your mind is this: If you think *'I'll do this – and then...'* – then don't do it.

'I'll do this – and then people will think I'm clever.'

'I'll do this – and then people will want me sexually.'

'I'll do this – and then I'll get likes followers subscribers job offers money power success happy sexy millionaire.'

It's counter-intuitive, as we see nobodies say nothing and apparently get money from it. 'I can say nothing too!', we think.

But don't. Although that's a double negative, so do? Anyway:

How can you know when it's right?

In reality; *if you don't even know why you're doing it* – do that!

Again, think back to historical works. Unlike our good friend Simon Sinek says, I bet they didn't *'start with why'*. Shakespeare certainly didn't have a 'why'. No one said "OK William I like the 'to be or not to be' but what's your WHY?"

No one said "Pyramids? But what's your WHY?!"

Knowing *why* won't necessarily make anything good. People can know why they do bad (evil or just dull) things too.

You might just not truly want to do it, or you might not be ready. Anyone who created anything good didn't do it until they did. This is about being the most YOU at any given time. Maybe it's your time to be soaking up information from what exists in the world. Or thinking. Or sleeping. None of these actions take away who you are: look at them as your creative 'side hustle'.

If you don't have a burning desire to do something then take the option of not doing the thing that you see everyone else doing.

If you are doing something but without reason, then don't feel the need to validate or explain yourself to anyone. The greatest creations or scientific discoveries in the world were often done in spite of, not with the approval of other people's opinions.

2. Get up and move

You could have most ideas better if you had them while walking or driving or at least pacing. Why are people referenced as pacing when thinking in archaic literature? Because it's natural and good.

Your home, or a boxy office room with a white board: two places that are not good for optimal creativity.

3. Build up a bank first

There's the creating part – and then there's the releasing it onto the world part, whether posting, publishing or showing in some way. How can you know if it's the right time to do that?

We humans are flighty things. Even if there was something that you had a burning desire to do or create – it might be temporary. That's not to say you shouldn't still go ahead and unleash it onto the world. The Beatles did their stuff in a famously short amount of time and The Godfather only needed two films to achieve immortality.

However, while it may be possible for you to achieve those levels, if you don't then it would be more beneficial for you to look long term. You can look at it this way: can you easily create a year's worth of whatever it is? Can you continue to release this to 'the public' for a matter of years?

This is only necessary due to how the modern world takes in information. If it's just one book you write then it would need to be so spectacular as to be a legend of prose, or it won't make a dent in the sphere of daily knowledge.

If it's a topic that you're talking about then if you only have 'a few' very good opinions then you might get bored of it yourself and change to something else (and then get bored of that yourself).

Of course, the caveat is as above – some people continue to create consistent crap, but they actually have lots of money (or their parents/partners do) and they pay PR agencies, publishers and the like to promote said crap.

What this is about is the power of specialisation – which is our next point!

4. Specialise in one thing

If you're thinking of starting something and it involves content – posting on a social media platform – then take your time to think of a specific angle; and then stick firmly to it. Do not self indulge your random opinions.

Few people have the personality to be general 'personalities' – even someone who does, like Jeremy Clarkson, started with just one specialisation.

I like watching the baker Paul Hollywood's TV programmes on bread, but I don't care what his favourite car or political leanings are.

I watch Richard Ayoade being glib and silly on a travel show but I know absolutely nothing about his personal life and that's just as I want it.

If you still feel like you can create more than one particular thing and aren't sure where to begin, give yourself confidence by following gut instinct and owning your ideas, not by trying to predict what other people will like.

5. Listen to other people and then do what you want anyway

If it's about being creative then it doesn't really matter what alleged statistics say or what other people think. Then you're not being creative, you're doing things to fit the narrow thinking of others, or just borrowing ideas from others.

To be honest you probably shouldn't listen to others, because they aren't you. Just don't tell anyone that you won't listen to them. People don't like that. They think it's arrogant. They think your thought is all about THEM. Which displays their mental weaknesses and why you shouldn't listen to them.

Listen, smile, nod – and then do what you believe in your gut is best.

It's fashionable to say things must have a strategy, or an end goal, or worse, a 'call to action', but real creativity is not dependent on any of these things.

If anyone tells you what 'best practice' is, then, my friend, you are speaking to a dullard robot.

You as an economic unit

This is what I saw on TV once:

A government politician - it just so happened to be a member of the Conservative party - was being interviewed on TV about unemployment. The host was asking him about the rise in unemployment and what he had to say about it.

The politician's response was to say that it wasn't actually about a rise in unemployment, because during the same time period, other people had also started employment. He said that yes, around 250,000 had gotten onto the unemployed status, but in the same time, around 200,000 moved onto employed status.

He said, and I quote: "it's about the churn." He then explained that there was a 'huge churn' in numbers of people who either were becoming unemployed or employed, so the whole thing should be seen from this perspective.

He had a wide-jawed head, and a red-ish, moist glow, as if he'd had whisky with his dinner before going on TV.

When he said "churn", he used one hand to make a large semi-circle churning motion. I don't know, but I wonder if, in his mind at that moment, hundreds of thousands of useless poor people were being churned round and round his gigantic and powerful palm.

At the end of their exchange, the host didn't follow up with any further questions, as usually happens on British TV. Either the TV host is too polite to really ask why the government is so incredibly shit at doing its job, or, perhaps they are being influenced behind the scenes. Or both? I have no idea.

But the point here is not the weakness and meekness and uselessness of political journalists on TV, it's that the phrase 'churn' was used so casually, and that these 'numbers' were not seen as individual human beingsl with lives. Just a churn of bodies that either were or were not employed in their hundreds of thousands.

This is how you are seen by government. Again, this isn't a late-age teenage strop against the powers that be and isn't the system whack man (or whatever teenagers say this year). It's a simple statement conveyed without emotion, based on the real words used by government politicians as they visualise a sea of desperate churning nobodies moving around columns on a non-existent spreadsheet.

It is worth keeping this in mind when making financial choices.

Put it alongside the 'sex sells' in advertising.

Even if you move past the manipulative aspect of internet connection advertising trying to manipulate your sexual juices into a purchase: do you think those companies using sex to sell even CARE whether you actually get the purported sex? No. Of course they do not. They see you as nothing but an economic unit.

We already know, based on actual evidence, that politicians see you as just being an immobile corpse that is CHURNED round and round on an endless cycle of plebian nothingness.

Do you think those 'brands' care about you, or how your purchase saves the polar bears due to its 100% recyclable (except the cap) bottle?

All the emotion that they wrap up into the persuasion is, I'm sorry to say, fake.

Thus, it helps one to make the purchases that are innately desired, or necessary.

This in turn helps you to have the control you need to have the internet connection provider that is best for being YOU, not best for helping you to find the love that the paid actors shared on screen for five seconds.

How to be the most argumentative you

Only in person

Making points by email or in an online comment has never once been known to work in the history of the online world. Recording things in black and white is different, and necessary. Recording what happened or making (emotion-free) statements is valuable by email, as it reduces hearsay and forces people to also record their points or statements in words, rather than anything they can deny or take back later.

But for something that is more akin to argument: at least go to a recorded video call, or you're just going to get more frustrated. The online comment is the worst of all of these, because the other person is making their post or point for one thing: attention. Any comment is giving them what they want.

Use the opportunity to agree with an accusation

If you agree with the person then you can take away their point. If someone uses a "you're only doing this because it's good for you" type of accusation, then you could calmly agree that yes you are trying to achieve what's right for you in this situation. If you calmly accept that and move on to your point, it has stopped them from turning the conversation away from what it is about.

Always hold back the strongest point

The course of an argument or debate will go on for a while. Two people or parties do not make one single point and then a decision is immediately made or conclusion arrived at. That would be nice, but people aren't so intelligent. They need to get their various egos and urges fulfilled.

Thus, there early pointers in any argument are usually dismissed, no matter what they are. Putting the best or strongest point out early on isn't best. Ace up the sleeve, trump card, save the best for last. The nonsense that people haven't thought out, or just things they want to voice: these are the things to let others fuss around with. When they have exhausted their voices or run out of things to say, putting in the strongest point can sometimes see people listen to that point itself rather than the ego-caring time when apparently everyone needs to be able to have their say, even if it's stupid and unhelpful.

Reduce volume

Which person do you think is the one that can be most f*cked with – the one shouting and gesticulating wildly – or the one in calm control, keeping her/his cool in even extreme circumstances?

Also, volume leaves you with nowhere else to go but down, at which point you just look silly for shouting in the first place.

People are inherently stupid and will like to be led – shouting at kids makes them shout back. Arguing in a state of calm would enforce the other person to also keep civility to the process and show their own volume or rage up as immature and a lack of self-control: weakness.

Phrase things as questions

Questions rather than statements. "What do you think people would say if you..." or "Do you think it's possible that people would get confused if you..." may be better than saying "What you have done is idiotic," or "You are a moron."

The least emotion

What is the least emotional way you can say something? Often it is by actually describing your emotions. "Why the fuck did you do that?" is emotional and often triggers an angry response that's about the other person's ego, but "Doing that made me feel..." has been known to reduce their ego and make them see the consequence of their actions.

The most professional you

This is where the most you is the controlled you. Even in the nicest job, you are still owned in some way, and thus cannot always be the most you, in reality.

The working world is a game. Adults play it, but many adults haven't progressed to complete maturity.

It's also unique in its transactional nature. It's openly transactional - you get paid X to do Y - but modern nonsense sees you also needing to show passion, teamwork, care and lots of other emotions.

LinkedIn is the biggest game of the professional world. No matter what nonsense you see, you can very rarely (if ever) gain professionally by honestly pointing out something you think is nonsense. If employment is money, you can only gain this by joining in with the game.

Of course it's nonsensical for any company selling products to also talk about sustainability. Only Patagonia comes close by going all the way to saying 'don't buy this jacket' as the only way to truly be 'sustainable'. All the other companies talk nonsense.

Believe it or not, McDonald's has a position of Chief Impact Officer. The factual impact of McDonald's is obesity and pollution. Their TV adverts put the onus on the consumer throwing away the rubbish after eating it, in a subtle greenwashing tactic. Yet if you were to say this on LinkedIn (I haven't), no one would care.

Yet if you were to comment "this is fantastic, great to see an iconic brand lead the way," then you could possibly increase your chances of employment and money.

The conflict in modern work comes from the hype of emotion. You could do your actual job and work tasks to a truly amazing standard but you still can't really cross the line and say "I don't care, this is just a job for me," because people don't like that.

The professional world needs another book of its own, and in this context we have to see the truth: that being the most you in the career world may mean playing the game cleverly and with a cheery eager smile that no one could really maintain for five days a week.

You and what's next

'OK, but what's next?'

This aspect of innate human questioning is a key driver of our species.

It likely happened when we evolved the hands we have today, along with the necessary abundant food which meant we had time to sit and think. Or I suppose you might just think 'God did it', if you're easily persuaded into things. Which God? That would entirely depend on where you grew up and who told you what was in fact true, when compared to all the other false ones. But I digress.

The 'OK, but what's next?' is funny because, as explained previously, it seems to be what humans thought about most once they had come to a realisation of 'what it means to be human' and 'how can we achieve harmony and peace of mind?'.

They pretty much got there, but then the other side of humanity decided it wasn't enough and they needed to keep warring and hoarding.

As we've mentioned in Freud's theory, put simply:

The id drives basic urges such as eating and mating and having some form of power.

The ego thinks about anything and everything that can be done to get these.

The superego thinks 'hang on a minute, let's be civilised about this'.

The interesting thing is that we can psychologically evolve (some of us) but we cannot negate the id, the animal.

We can muse and mull and opine and be empathetic and do good, but our body will continue to create hormones that feed the id. I'm not advocating chemical castration on mass, and there are of course controls and ways to channel the id, such as using cutlery to eat and monogamy to do relationships with.

But that only works for some people. Other people biologically lack the brain capacity to listen to their own brain, and thus a certain percentage of the mass of humanity remains id-based.

Whatever your capacity for living well with the various parts of your brain, it's interesting because it means that the realisation is that it is OK to think 'OK but what's next?'.

And not just because I say so and I'm a man, but because it has been proven in human history.

Most or all of the advice or thoughts or guidance around mental and whole wellbeing leads you toward the reflection, the introspection, the 'being healthy'. These things are good, from this angle, but they often lead to 'yes I know this but I don't actually do it'.

This might be because the assumption is that people want to be healthy in these ways.

But the body's chemicals seem to get either confused or bored if the pinnacle of health is seen as harmony and peace and calm.

Why don't people like healthy food? Even if it tastes good, it doesn't spike the brain the same way that other foods do; foods such as beef, cheese, coffee, chocolate, spice (which can have health benefits in some ways) and sugar, animal fat and fried vegetable fat.

So we know what food will be 'healthy', but many or most people find it difficult to not eat unhealthy food, even if it is continually wrapping itself round and round their bodies in a thick layer of coating fat. That's their choice and not a judgement on that except from the angle of potential body problems.

We all fully know this about food, but the same isn't quite true of life situations.

There is a greater assumption that people 'want a healthy life' rather than people seek out, if subconsciously, some form of warring and hoarding, whatever that may be for them.

So, let's first look at some similarities between the effects of stimulating food and the natural release of feel-good hormones in the brain:

Activation of reward pathways:

When a person consumes stimulating food or experiences the release of feel-good hormones, the brain's reward pathways, particularly the mesolimbic pathway, become activated. This pathway involves the release of the neurotransmitter dopamine in specific brain regions, such as the nucleus accumbens.

Stimulating Food: Consuming stimulating food activates the brain's reward circuitry through various mechanisms. For example, the taste buds on the tongue detect the sensory properties of food, and this information is transmitted to the brain via the gustatory system. The brain interprets these sensory signals and triggers the release of dopamine in the nucleus accumbens, which contributes to feelings of pleasure and reward.

Feel-Good Hormones: The release of feel-good hormones, such as oxytocin, dopamine, adrenaline, and cortisol, can also activate the brain's reward pathways. For instance, dopamine plays a key role in reward processing and is released in response to pleasurable experiences, reinforcing positive behaviours. Oxytocin, often referred to as the "bonding hormone," is released during social interactions and can promote feelings of trust and wellbeing. Adrenaline and cortisol are stress hormones that, when released in appropriate amounts, can enhance arousal and focus.

Pleasurable sensations:

Both stimulating food and the natural release of feel-good hormones can evoke pleasurable sensations, albeit through different mechanisms.

Stimulating Food: Consuming stimulating food can directly stimulate taste receptors on the tongue. These receptors detect the basic tastes (sweet, salty, sour, bitter, umami) and transmit signals to the brain via the gustatory system. The brain processes these taste signals and integrates them with other sensory information to create a pleasurable experience. Additionally, certain nutrients found in stimulating food, such as sugar and fat, can also trigger the release of opioids in the brain, contributing to a sense of pleasure.

Feel-Good Hormones: The release of feel-good hormones can induce pleasurable sensations through their effects on the brain. For example, dopamine, when released in response to rewarding stimuli, can create a sense of pleasure and reinforce behaviours that lead to its release. Oxytocin, besides its role in social bonding, can promote feelings of calmness and contentment. Adrenaline, also known as epinephrine, is involved in the body's stress response and can induce feelings of heightened alertness and excitement. Cortisol, another stress hormone, is released during challenging situations and can influence arousal and focus.

Motivation and reinforcement:

Both stimulating food and the release of feel-good hormones can act as motivators and reinforce certain behaviours.

Stimulating Food: Consuming stimulating food can trigger a pleasurable response in the brain, reinforcing the behaviour of seeking out similar food in the future. This reinforcement can occur through the activation of the brain's reward pathways and the release of dopamine. Over time, this association between consuming stimulating food and the ensuing pleasure can lead to cravings and the motivation to seek out those foods again.

Feel-Good Hormones: The release of feel-good hormones can also play a role in motivation and reinforcement. When certain activities or experiences lead to the release of these hormones, they can create a positive association and reinforce it. For instance, engaging in social interactions and experiencing the release of oxytocin can motivate individuals to seek out more social connections. Dopamine release in response to achieving goals or experiencing rewards can reinforce things that contribute to such outcomes.

So:

It's worth thinking about your relationship with life situations from a similar angle as your relationship with food. You probably understand the pull of 'unhealthy' food, try to be healthy but opt for some indulgence now and then. That's a safe generalisation for most humans because it does not have prescriptive boundaries. Very few people truly 'eat clean' 100% of the time, and few (yet more) only eat ridiculously unhealthily 100% of the time.

But what if you are subconsciously doing something similar in other areas of life? Such as you try to be a 'good employee' but subconsciously act like a twat for 5% (or whatever) of the time because your brain (not 'you) is driving you toward some hormones and not always in a positive sense?

Ditto relationships of the romantic kind and accidentally-on-purpose being a dick?

It's different to self-sabotage, which can happen when an individual has specific fear, often borne from situations in formative years. This leads to either fear of failure, fear of success, low self-esteem or overly high goal-setting.

It's something else that can happen to anyone, because anyone/everyone has the animal inside.

How does this relate to our context of the whole you?

Like this:

1. You feel like you haven't been able to live as or become the 'most you'

2. To achieve this, you recognise that changes need to be made in how you live

3. The 'wellbeing' or life/success guidance that you've seen tells you to just 'do things'

4. You tried doing the things but lost motivation for many possible reasons

5. And repeat

So what was missing?

If we go back to the start of the book and see that humans came to forms of solidly logical reasoning of how to live well,

161

we see that for most people, it felt insufficient, as explained above.

This is because it didn't offer a pay off.

The percentage of people whose brains can accept being true monks is minimal. Unless you have a monk-type brain, your brain will be looking for the pay off.

The pay off in food, or the pay off in social situations.

There's no clear pay off in most proffered 'solutions'. You can read the list of lots of "Habits of Highly Effective People" but that just sounds like hard work from the outside, and, one of the steps is 'make a plan', I mean DUH, for want of a better literary critique.

So based on the sections of you / this book:

Your mind:

When do you like your mind most?

If the answer is 'all the time' then I'd say that you need to share with the world how you achieved this.

Otherwise, try to harness those times when you like your mind the most. See how you can create expression due to those times.

What can you do each day that triggers that state? What can you do to share those moments? Is it meeting others who are conducive to this state, or actually making an effort to play a sport or join a community that allows you to express yourself in any physical (and therefore whole) way?

Your heart:

What kind of feelings do you like to have each day?

This might sound silly, if you assume that people want good feelings. But I hope that we have pushed all assumptions away by now.

I once heard someone say "I don't think about it, because I don't like to be angry."

This might sound impossible to achieve for the over-thinker, but the simple will to hold onto what you like to feel and reject what you don't like to feel seems to make sense.

It goes against the usual advice because we should apparently overturn and analyse every single emotion, but 'life's too short' seems a much more sensible phrase than any other I can think of right now.

Your gut:

Do you listen to your nous and intuition?

If you feel like weighing up the various choices you've made in life, which did you make with your gut feel?

How did those ones turn out versus the others when you felt like you 'should' do something for or due to others/society?

Your genitals:

What are your methods for dealing with your sexuality?

In terms of awareness, do you feel repressed? This is unsurprisingly the most 'personal' question or area that we are dealing with, but it's a question that each person should feel free to ask themselves and see what answers arise.

And without context...

How would you answer these questions if you weren't living in our present time?

What is the you that was born and had the innate 'nature' part?

What if you had been 'nurtured' differently in another time/place?

That question is about the potential that lies within.

Now, of course our formative years define some of our beliefs and abilities due to the spongelike aspect of a child's brain and the creation of neuro-things (such as you can learn to play the piano more easily when young).

However, the nature versus nurture debate is slightly limited due to the word 'nurture'.

What if the 'nature' part can always be nurtured to some degree?

This way, the person that you are now hasn't been fixed and there is no need to look back and think' if only my parents had pushed me to learn ice skating' or something.

Whatever the specifics, it is unlikely that your nurture was able to fully uncover the complete nature within you.

Unless you're a child, you're not really being 'nurtured' now, and perhaps you can continually nurture yourself by learning and so forth.

But if you look at your 'nature', what is that?

It is the way you are and the way you want to live, the things you want to do. Hopefully, if you look at that in isolation, those are good things.

If you bring that back to the context of modern times, then think about anything you do not like, anything that gets in your nature's way.

Maybe they are things like stress, anxiety, concern, impatience, frustration, perhaps caused by things like: the fixed daily schedule/routine, traffic, money worries, peer pressure.

Those things are more the 'nurture' you are experiencing now.

So: if you have available to you now a list of things that nurture you - and you still feel like they are hindering, restricting, frustrating the most natural you inside, then alternatives seem to be the strong combative effect.

If the world of self-help / development / learning / growing / achieving has still not led to the most you being unleashed, then what about drastic reversal?

164

1. Try Two Mentors

The mentorship thing has always sounded weird to me, because it assumes full (or at least partial) deference to another human being who, despite perhaps having the kind of success you want, is indeed another human and therefore irrelevant to the very specific journey on which you are going.

So a 'mentor' could simply be someone that you admire from afar and see how you can kind of do what they did to get the result they achieved.

What if you had a mentor (in direct or from afar context) who hasn't necessarily achieved these things but is from a younger generation, and therefore less encumbered by the things that are nurturing you in your current life stage?

Maybe this simply means looking at a happy child or stupid animal and living the way they do each day in order to feel happy? No idea. I mean I wrote this book but I DON'T HAVE ALL THE ANSWERS, JESUS!

That was childish. And I liked it.

2. Have a Selfish Plan

See, I can say 'have a plan'! That Covey fellow sold a billion books by telling people 'have a plan', so I'm copying that to get the same success.

Except, not really. What if... all the wellbeing or success stuff says to take small steps, be mindful, set goals, find support blah blah blah, BUT the actual so-called rich and powerful and cool did NONE of these things to get their success?

Now I can't advocate fully doing things that others did such as nepotism, self-obsession, hoarding, scheming, or simply 'be born a Prince', but, what if you label a plan honestly?

What if you mentally labelled it with the thing that you secretly want but could never say on LinkedIn (money or sex or something) in order to motivate yourself to do the small actions needed, by keeping the pay off front, centre and top of the plan?

3. Go Off Menu

'Off menu' is one of the most pretentious and sickening little social media things possible.

What happens is that someone goes to a restaurant, posts their photos of their food and then - specifically - states that one of the dishes was 'off menu'.

"OMG the dishes at Restaurant Twatto were amazeballs, NGL. We had the truffled truffle with truffles, the picanha steak with harissa and the gochujang cloud bread (off menu). Thanks for the special arrangement, person we know who works there!"

I mean really, "(off menu)". The HEIGHT of modern ego nonsense it takes to need to inform other people that you had a dish that was not on the menu for norms and dullards. The shit menu. Frankly fuck the menu and I only go to restaurants to not eat what they said they serve.

Anyway: the point is that I have used this to exorcise those particular personal demons AND hypothesise that you do something a bit differently from the way that you normally see your expected expectations.

I don't mean something like 'buy a gun and...', but more like this:

I was walking into a supermarket some time this year and walking out was a man. He seemed to be wearing cycling-type clothing, not that that's relevant.

He saw me and said "Good morning! It's wonderful weather we're having today, isn't it!!!" in a cheery and effusive voice.

I said 'oh yes it is' or something, and while this didn't particularly thrill me personally because of various reasons, it seems like a nice way to connect with strangers and potentially offer a stranger a different and refreshing moment in an otherwise drab second.

I'm sure you have had moments in public where, not exactly that, but you have perhaps seen 'something' and thought to yourself 'maybe I should... help / say [this] / do [something]'.

What if you ensured you did that more regularly?

4. Be seasonal

It should be recognised that you can only be the most you sometimes. The most you was never ALL the time.

Or, put it this way, the most you is recognising that during the last week of November when the weather is bad is only really good for staying in and watching TV.

It's incredibly difficult to not go along with nature, especially as nurture as intertwined and concluded that Summer is X and Winter is Y and the Sun makes you happy and no one really does much in February except be thankful it's not January anymore.

What society does is push you to the short term a little.

Firstly, we were told (and accepted) January is 'new year new you'.

Then we realised that this pushes pressure onto January and people set resolutions that they never reach.

Do you see that this pushes your eyes down to navel-gazing over what you're doing for just a matter of months?

Instead, what if anything you did for yourself, during any month, was 'for next year' or for two years away? Or more?

There's also the aspect - seasonally speaking - of finding joy in each season: living in celebration of the highlights that each season holds. That's something that is run by nature, not man, and is therefore outside of the constructed world of conflict and control.

TO CONCLUDE

In Conclusion

There are decent people in the world, there are bad people in the world. Even decent people can be bad sometimes. Bad people want two things: power and attention.

Good people still want power, but on balance they can either control their avarice for it, or they would actually wish to use power as a vehicle for doing good rather than the crave of power itself. Most likely the former.

When you remove all the fluff, people want power. Even money comes under the category of power. The second category - attention - is absolutely a kind of power, but it's different.

Money is a very pragmatic kind of power. Attention is an emotional power, and the number one thing that some people want.

It's when people realised that children behave badly because they want any kind of attention, even discipline and blame.

This is all about other people yet, precluding the notion that you, the reader, is a power-hungry attention-whore, you will still want some power and attention, because humans are now hyper-survivalists.

As a species, we are in effect too good at surviving.

We know that our bodies haven't evolved as fast as our minds, which is why we still crave fat and our bodies cling onto it in case there is no food tomorrow or we need to run from danger.

Moreover, we still chase survival-type things in a mental sense.

Convenience comes under the category of survival. We want ever increasing convenience, to modern-day ridiculous levels and, if we don't get it, we go instantaneously to extreme reactions of anger and frustration.

Storytelling has been popular since cavepeople's time.

Stories take out all of the stodge and boredom of a normal sequence of events and give you the highlights.

Stories leave out the bit where the character just kind of waited around or spent time negotiating with a particularly difficult bowel movement.

Movies and now social media offer the stories of highlight, with the latter instantly accessible.

The dopamine hit of stories meets the fear-mongering of the power-insane and causes a background adrenalisation with a cortisol undertone.

Even supposed 'mental health messaging' tells you that it's OK not to be successful in one big step but that you can take many steps. The background still suggests that success is absolutely the destination you must reach though.

Essentially, you may have everything you need in life but from waking to sleeping, you are being told about the infinite universe of more. Or, you don't have it but it looks like everyone else has.

That is the background to present day life.

So how can you combat this?

Looking at what manipulation the inputs you receive have on your mind, heart, gut and genitals may be one way to compartmentalise the various parts that make up the whole you.

Remember that our premise of 'the most you' means the one you see as the 'most good' (not 'best') and the real you that would exist anywhere on Earth if at any time on Earth.

It doesn't mean 'doing the most', as being the most you could be deciding that inaction is your best course.

Ipso facto as we look at the personal compartments of your self, first off it gives you a choice of what range you decide to pick at any given moment:

The mind:

Do you feel in control of your thoughts in the moment? Do you weigh up that your thoughts may either be partially or fully brought on by the controlling external stimulus of others, be that the controlling elite or the conflicted others?

The heart:

How emotionally invested are you - truly - in the things your 'heart' (emotional mind) is telling you? Have you been groomed into thinking this way? And even if it is genuine love, how willing are you to take the actions that love is pushing you to do? A parent can love her/his child but there still needs to be boundaries, for the sake of both the parent and the child's energy levels. And as seen in sayings that stood the test of time, love needs some time and space to decrease rather than remain at highest pitch.

The gut:

How much do you listen to your gut feel and intuition? Do you go through the day mainly living in 'the mind' as we see it here? Or mainly in the other self components? Your gut is the one that has a confident background voice and more of a 'hang on a minute' vibe to it. Do you feed your gut with the nutrition it needs to work in sync with the mind?

The genitals:

What is your balance of openness, repression and mind realisation of the power of your hormones over your daily or life actions?

So:

As a conclusion within a conclusion, from this context it's your gut that is the most you of the most you.

The nous, intuition, instinct, gut feel: these are the aspects which seem less disturbed by the conflicted and controlling external world.

And?

The rest is, if anything, the easy part.

We've spent around 50,000 words looking at lots of things, but to finish with a reduced jus of nutritional bookish goodness, we can conclude the conclusion with the focus back on the important person here: me. Just kidding! It's you.

After looking with a healthy dose of cynicism at the purported tools of definitive mental goodness - such as introspection and mindfulness - let's look at the things which do seem to work for people who are most at one with themselves.

1:An adult purpose

This doesn't have to be anything exceptionally unique, and it can change whenever you want it to. You can have more than one.

I say 'an adult purpose' because it has to emphasise that an adult realises the context of themselves as an individual in just one relatively nanoscopic moment on Earth. People who don't realise this are childish and very often world leaders.

But as a purpose of an individual living one standard life in the world, it helps you to have a background hum of confidence.

If your purpose is, let's say, raising your children, then it is a grounding realisation that stops you doing silly things, such as being angry about the minutiae of daily life.

Maybe you've already done the raising children part of life. Without the finding and founding of a new purpose then you may be stuck in the empty nest syndrome, with a loss of motivation or direction. A renewed purpose could be anything that brings back the groove to life.

If your purpose is, let's say, being part of a business or organisation that does 'some form of good' in the world, then it can give you the solace that, despite the continued destruction of the planet by others, you are doing what small bit you are able to do.

Even if you have sub-purposes of, let's say, going on holiday to the Maldives, then it is a continued reminder that the small improvements you make to either your bank balance or daily choices are actually building up to something else.

Whatever the purpose is, it's the all-important compass that remains clear and true during the choppy waters.

2: Time

Time away! Away from others, from life. Time away from those you love most is still good for you. So, imagine the power that you get from taking time away from the things you aren't keen on.

This is, of course, well known as 'a holiday', but we are usually programmed into only being apportioned a tiny amount of this. For example people are either ensnared by the school term routine, or even if mainly at work, they are allotted less than 10% of the year to not be a productive slave making money for people 'above' them who already have lots, lots more of it.

Aside from changing your entire job or lifestyle, we still have 'spend more time in nature' as the ultimate get away which doesn't need a full week's vacation.

If we want you to have some experience of the 'you at any time or place on Earth' then this you can only really be accessed when in nature. This is the you away from buildings, roads, cars, TVs, modern things - including 'modern day people' and their modern day noise.

Realistically you will still take your phone with you but I have to trust that you won't be one of those odd people who looks at their phone when slap bang in nature itself.

This time, whether a week/day/hour away from others is sacred and a regular need, akin to brushing your teeth or having your morning drink.

3: Patience

"And then the main character was really patient and waited for some years, then later the thing they wanted to happen happened" - said no story ever.

It would make quite the shit story but as real life isn't a dopamine-inducing queue of dominoing highlights, the things you want might take fifteen years (or something) to happen.

4: I think that's it

As mentioned, it's a simple list for a simple person: you.

You might possibly be surprised at this point that there isn't much 'health' advice or content given to the point of being the most you.

Yes, of course from some perspectives, you will be able to be the most you if you have the most energy. This energy would be a result of sleeping well, eating lots of fruits and vegetables (and also carbohydrates and nutrient-rich proteins such as beef), and exercising.

But that's prescriptive and assumptive.

And possibly a topic for another book.

Thanks for reading.

Bye you.

About The Author

@NickWithycombe

Also:

How To Be Free From Concern - available on Amazon and
Apple Books

Printed in Great Britain
by Amazon

27905195R00106